1st edition

THE

Busy Family's Guide to

Estate Planning

10 Steps to Peace of Mind

by Attorney Liza Weiman Hanks

NOLO

First Edition	MAY 2007
Editor	MARY RANDOLPH
Book Design	TERRI HEARSH
Cover Design	SUSAN WIGHT
Proofreading	JOE SADUSKY
Index	THÉRÈSE SHERE
Printing	DELTA PRINTING SOLUTIONS, INC.

Hanks, Liza Weiman, 1961 -

The busy family's guide to estate planning : 10 steps to peace of mind
by Liza Weiman Hanks.

p. cm.

ISBN-13: 978-1-4133-0634-7 (pbk.)

ISBN-10: 1-4133-0634-9 (pbk.)

1. Estate planning--United States--Popular works. I. Title

KF750.Z9H32 2007

332.024'016—dc22

2006039254

For information on bulk purchases or corporate premium sales, please contact the Special Sales department. For academic sales or textbook adoptions, ask for Academic Sales. Call 800-955-4775 or write to Nolo at 950 Parker St., Berkeley, CA 94710.

Dedication

To Leslie A. Barton, in loving memory.

Acknowledgments

Steven, Kate, and Sam Hanks, my family, for their support, patience, and collective sense of humor.

Mary Randolph, the best editor I have ever had the pleasure of working with, for always making this book better.

Diane Brown, Naomi Comfort, Tish Loeb, Matt Wesley, and Carol Zolla, my estate planning colleagues, who have taught me so much.

Corinne Taylor, my friend and assistant, for keeping my law practice running so smoothly while I wrote this book.

About the Author

Liza Weiman Hanks is an attorney and the founder of FamilyWorks Estate Planning, a practice specializing in estate planning for families. A graduate of Stanford Law School, she has also served as an instructor at the Santa Clara University Law School and practiced with the state of California and a prestigious Silicon Valley firm. Liza lives with her family in Campbell, California.

Table of Contents

4 Make Your Will

5 Consider a Living Trust

6 Name the Right Beneficiaries for Your Retirement Plans

7 Get Enough Life Insurance

Index

CD-ROM

Forms

The Ideal Guardian

Potential Guardians

Guardians for My Children

Family Inventory

My Children's Money Managers

Audio Files

Your Estate Planning Companion

Any parent knows that it isn't easy keeping a busy family running smoothly. Just getting through the *day* sometimes feels like more than we can handle: juggling daycare, doctors, school, and activities, with a dash of sibling rivalry thrown in to make it all as chaotic as possible. If you've picked up this book, though, you also know that you have more to plan for than day-to-day life. There are long-term financial and legal things to think about, too.

Making those long-term plans is called "estate planning." And it's not that hard. Unless you're very wealthy, you don't need to create lots of complicated legal documents to avoid paying taxes. It's a pretty straightforward process, and this book explains it. In ten chapters, in fact, you'll make your complete estate plan.

If you've tried to get an estate plan done in the past but stopped halfway through, or you've just avoided the topic carefully since your kids were born, don't feel bad. You're in good company. Most people haven't done any estate planning at all. If you think I'm wrong, try this: The next time you pick your kids up from school, ask your friends whether they've done an estate plan. You'll see what I mean. (Then give them this book.)

Estate planning means making important decisions for the people you love. If you don't do it, it means that someone else (a judge) would make critical decisions about your children's future if you died unexpectedly. Putting things in place now means you keep control over what would happen. You can't control fate, but you can plan for it, and by doing so, you'll find that your mind is more at ease.

As an estate planner, my motto is, "Feel Good, Not Guilty." Stop worrying about what you haven't done and get to work. This book breaks estate planning down into ten manageable chunks, so that you don't have to face everything at once. Each chapter walks you through the essential things you must do to create a comprehensive family estate plan. It includes a simple will form and explains how to find and complete all the other documents you'll need. Even if you do one chapter a month (and take August and December off), by this time next year, you'll be done!

Of course, you might not *want* to do all your own estate planning; after all, you've got a lot on your plate already. That's fine—not everyone wants to do their own taxes or change their own oil, either. If so, use this guide as a workbook to make your work with an estate planning attorney easier and more efficient.

This book explains how to:

- understand what your family owns
- plan for your children, so that if you die before they grow up, they'll be raised by people you love and respect
- manage your children's inheritance, so that they won't be in charge of any money you leave them until they're responsible adults
- complete a will or a living trust to make your choices legally binding
- review your retirement plans and life insurance policies to make sure that you're leaving enough and leaving it to the right people, and
- choose people to make critical health care and financial decisions for you if you can't.

Although basic estate planning isn't legally complicated, it's emotionally difficult. That's really why most of us put it off. If the very thought of completing the process makes you want to end it all, don't despair. This book is intended to be your legal companion, providing practical and supportive advice and information along the way.

When you're done, you'll know that you've done one of the most caring things you can do as a parent: ensure that should you no longer be able to care for you children, you'll have left them in good hands, with enough money, and with a competent plan to manage that money for them until they're able to manage it for themselves.

Choose Guardians for Your Children

· ·

What you'll do here:

☐ Identify the qualities and values that matter most to you in a guardian.

☐ Brainstorm a list of potential guardians.

☐ Identify three guardians from that list.

· ·

Picking trusted adults who will take care of your children if you can't is the most important estate planning task on your list as a parent.

And for many parents, picking guardians for their children is also by far the hardest thing about making an estate plan. Somehow, just thinking about the possibility that we won't be here to raise our kids seems to make it more likely that it could actually happen. Intellectually, we know that's nonsense—but it's still a distasteful task.

Don't put if off, though. If a child has two parents, and one dies, the survivor carries on as the sole parent. But if both parents die together, or if a single parent dies or can't raise a child, someone must be legally responsible for the child. That person is known as the child's personal guardian and is appointed by a judge in a probate court proceeding. Unless you put your wishes in writing, the judge will have to choose a guardian without any idea of whom you wanted to raise your children.

Get It Done

Choosing guardians is never easy. But it is too important a decision to leave to a stranger. You need to know that you're doing the best you can in selecting people who could provide a loving home for your kids. And keep in mind that making a choice that works for the next three to five years is much better than doing nothing at all. You can—and should—reevaluate your decisions in five years, anyway. As your children grow and your relationships with family and friends change, your guardianship choices may very well change, too.

For many of my estate planning clients, the difficulty of picking a guardian is the single biggest reason for not getting their estate planning done. There are just so many good reasons not to do the work it takes: There's no time to have that conversation with your spouse or partner; there are no good choices among friends and family; it's just too hard to think about the unlikely scenario of dying while your kids are young. Still, all of these reasons often just boil down to the fact that it's emotionally too wrenching to imagine needing a guardian, let alone naming one, or two, or three.

If you're feeling that way, here are some ways to get the job done. First, tell yourself that this is like having fire insurance, making sure you have an earthquake preparedness kit in the back shed, or drawing up a basic hurricane evacuation plan. You'll probably never need to use your emergency preparations, but if you ever do, your family will be so pleased that you cared enough about them to plan ahead.

Second, remind yourself that sometimes being a parent means you have to be brave and do the right thing, even when it is a bit difficult—you take your kids to the doctor to get their shots (okay, they hated it more than you did, but it was hard, wasn't it?), you buckle them into their car seats even when they're writhing and screaming, and you always make sure that their teeth are brushed.

And third, you just might discover, as many of my clients have, that making an estate plan actually reduces your anxiety about dying. There's something about making a contingency plan that can be comforting. You still can't control untimely fate, but you can be secure in knowing that you've done everything you can to make sure that your children would be safe and well cared for if the unexpected did happen. So think hard about estate planning for a while, and once you're done, move on to other, more rewarding plans, like your next vacation or how to redo the living room.

What About Godparents?

Godparents are important people in many children's religious lives. But they have no special legal standing. If you want to nominate your children's godparent as a guardian, you must do so in your will.

How Guardianships Work

Your job as a parent is to choose the people whom you would want to serve as guardians and to write those choices into your will. It's a judge's job, however, to give the people you've chosen the legal authority to serve as guardians, if it's ever necessary.

Judges give the people you name in your will priority over anyone else. A court would still, however, need to make sure that your nominated guardians would do a good job. In most states, that means that there would be a court-ordered investigation of the prospective guardian's background and home before the judge made the formal appointment. These investigations vary from state to state (and even within counties) but generally include an interview with a social worker, a background check, and a home visit. The social worker would then file a report to the judge about the suitability of the nominated guardian.

If you hadn't appointed a guardian in your will, or if you died without a will at all, then it would be the judge's job to select and appoint someone. The specific factors that judges must consider are determined by state law, but generally the list is sensible and includes items like these:

- the love and affection between the child and the proposed guardian
- the capacity of the proposed guardian to provide a loving, stable home
- the mental and physical health of the proposed guardian
- the guardian's moral fitness, and
- the child's preference.

In most cases where there's no will, a family member comes forward and requests to be named as guardian. If the judge determines the person who has come forward would take good care of the child, the judge will go ahead with the appointment.

What Guardians Are (and Are Not) Responsible For

A guardian has the legal authority and responsibility to care for a child, just as a parent does. The guardian's job is to provide a child's food, shelter, education, and medical care and to ensure their safety, security, and comfort until the child turns 18. And guardians, like parents, are legally responsible if a child under their control hurts another person or their property because they didn't supervise them properly.

> **EXAMPLE:** Katherine is the guardian of her 10-year-old niece, Shelby. Shelby had to move from her home in Idaho to Katherine's home in Oregon after her parents passed away. Katherine is responsible for making sure that Shelby gets to school every day and is well fed and well taken care of. If Shelby is having difficulty adjusting to her new school, it is Katherine's job to call the principal, discuss matters with Shelby's teachers, and take any other action that would be appropriate for a parent to take in the same situation.

Legal responsibilities aside, guardians, like parents, also end up having a lot of influence over the small day-to-day things that a child experiences. If your child is ever cared for by a guardian, the guardian will be the one to decide which movies your children watch, which activities they engage in, which food they eat (and don't), and whom they spend time with. Guardians would also have a role to play in the big decisions your children will make: where to go to college, what kind of jobs to take, and whom to marry.

By and large, once a personal guardian has been appointed, the court steps out of the picture and does not supervise the situation closely. Generally, a guardian must file annual status reports with the courts, reviewing how well the children are doing and where they're living and alerting the court to any changes that have occurred since the guardian was appointed.

State law determines the rules, but there are a few things that usually require the guardian to get the court's approval. For example, a guardian would need to get court permission before moving a child out of state. And a family member who felt that a guardian wasn't taking adequate care of a child could ask the court to terminate the guardianship and appoint someone else.

Although guardians are responsible for the general safety and well-being of the minor children in their care, usually called wards, they are not legally responsible for their wards' financial support. What that means is that guardians don't have to spend their own money to take care of their wards and can apply for public assistance programs on behalf of them.

Your children, though, won't ever be in that situation, because you are doing important financial planning for them right now. Your life insurance policies (see Chapter 7) will make sure that there would be enough money to take care of any minor children you left behind, and the person you've chosen to manage the proceeds (see Chapter 3) will make sure there's enough money for them until they turn 18 and hopefully long after that.

Parents can, and often do, leave money to the guardians in their wills, as a gift. A guardian, for example, might use such a gift to remodel a house and build an extra bedroom, buy a new car, or cut back on paid work to stay home and take care of small children. (You'll be thinking this issue through in Chapter 4, when you make your will.)

Picking the Right Guardian

You know that there is no one on the face of the earth capable of fully replacing you as a parent. Still, you've got to do the best you can. So next you will pick two, and preferably three, people to nominate as guardians. These are people who you believe will be able to give your children a loving home and get them to school, to the doctor, and anywhere else they need to be, until they are legal adults. You're going to choose more than one person because you want to make sure that just in case your first choice isn't available if the need ever arises, you have a backup or two.

The Ideal Guardian

The first step in choosing a guardian for your child is to sit down and write out the qualities that you'd like to find in your ideal guardian. Put down as many as you can think of. Then rank each of these qualities on a scale of 1 to 10. (You can assign the same rank to more than one quality.) Although you aren't likely to find all those qualities in any one person—possibly not even in yourself—your list will help you see which qualities you are willing to compromise on and which ones are not negotiable.

If you are raising your child with the other parent, it's a good idea for each of you to start by making a separate list. That way, each of you will be able to think about what matters most to you as an individual. After you've come up with your lists, you can compare them and see whether you can agree on at least the most important guardianship qualities and values. Your first lists may look very different—but don't see the divorce lawyer yet. It may take some time and effort, but you'll almost certainly be able to agree on a few important qualities, if not all.

Even though you and the other parent will each make your own separate will, it's important to pick the same guardians, so that there's no confusion about what you both wanted for your children. Even divorced parents, if they can communicate amicably, should try and pick the same guardians for their children.

The best reason to do this is that many children want to know who they would go to if there were an accident; it gives them a feeling of security. And it's nice for them to know that both parents agree on these choices. It also prevents confusion over whom to

The Ideal Guardian: An Example

Quality	Why It's Important to Me	Rank (10=essential; 1=no big deal)
Patience	A parenting skill required on a daily basis.	10
Sense of humor	An even MORE important parenting skill.	10
Enough money	To take care of my children's needs.	8
Spiritual outlook/ religious affiliation like mine	To give my children perspective.	6
Has children	To give my children companions.	3
Doesn't have children	To give my children adequate attention.	3
Member of my family	So that they stay close to grandparents and other relatives.	1
Lives close by	So that my children don't have to move far from their friends.	6
Loved by my children	Because my children need to be happy.	10
Values education	So that my children complete college.	7
Lives a healthy lifestyle	So that my children learn to eat and exercise properly.	7
Is politically aware and active	Because I am, and it is important to me that my children learn to be activists.	3
Loves sports	Because I love sports and they have been important in my life.	6
Reads all the time	Because I do.	7

name as a guardian if parents name different people in their wills and then die at the same time.

If parents don't die at the same time, the surviving parent's will controls where the children would go next—so the last parent surviving is the one who really has control over guardianship. But naming the same guardians avoids the possibility of an ugly challenge to a guardianship appointment at the second parent's death by the people named in the first parent's will.

An example of how Judy, a single mom with three children, ranked what was important to her is shown below. (A blank copy of this worksheet is in the Busy Family's Toolkit, on the CD-ROM that comes with this book.)

Making Your List

After you've listed the qualities and values that matter the most to you, your next job is to try to identify people who possess some of them and could serve as guardians. Again, each parent should make a list and then compare it with the other's. For now, just brainstorm all the likely possibilities without analyzing or eliminating, even though all of your candidates will probably fall short in one important way or another. (If you can't think of anyone, take a look at "Common Problems and Some Solutions," below, for help.)

When you make your list, think of individuals, not couples. If you want to name a couple to serve as guardians together, you can do that. But if they were ever to split up after being appointed as guardians, one of them would have to resign as guardian or they'd have to negotiate what would happen to your children as part of their divorce settlement. In the worst case, your children could be the subject of a custody fight. To avoid that, you can name just one person who would remain the guardian even if there were a divorce.

You can, however, always change your mind about a guardian and change your will accordingly. So, if you name a married couple as guardians, but they get divorced (or you change your mind for any other reason), you can always select a new guardian.

An example of the list that Judy came up with is shown below.

Potential Guardians: An Example

Person	Best Quality/Value	Major Drawbacks
Sister Anne	Very patient; kids love her.	Lives across the country.
Friend Carl	Spiritually like me; funny.	Single, not living in one place long. Doesn't live a healthy lifestyle.
Brother Joe and sister-in-law Alicia	Lives nearby; kids love them; big dog to play with; she coaches soccer and volleyball.	Small house; struggling financially; will have their own children soon.
My parents	Financially well-off; patient; close to the children.	In late 70s; no other children nearby. I don't like their politics.
Sister Emily	Financially well-off; funny; patient; shares my religion.	Her husband is not someone that I want my children to live with.
Brother-in-law Charles and sister-in-law Christine	They have two kids close in age to mine; they're both patient and kind.	Live in another country.
Friend Madeline	My kids love her; has three children and many cats and dogs; funny and patient; values education highly.	Bad at managing money.

Narrowing Down Your Choices

Having identified the values that matter most to you and made a list of the people in your life, it is time to narrow your choices. First, cross off anyone on either parent's list whose drawbacks are just too big.

EXAMPLE: Because Judy would not want her children to live with her sister Emily's husband, she crosses Emily off her potential guardian's list. She also crosses off her sister Anne, who lives across the country—Judy's oldest child is just beginning middle school, and moving so far away from his friends seems like too much of a burden to put on him. Finally, she crosses of her parents. Much as she loves them, and much as her children love them, she doesn't feel that two people in their late 70s should, or could, raise three active children.

Now you're probably getting down to the final few people on your lists. If, at this point, you feel like giving up completely, hang in there. Remember, no one on earth can replace you as a parent (even if there are times when your kids think that pretty much anyone else on earth would do). Choosing a guardian is always a second-best choice, but it is still one that you can make better than anyone else. Take a look back at your list of qualities and values and focus on the qualities that you ranked as a 9 or 10.

Now, try to choose two or three people from the names remaining on the list who bring at least one, if not more, of your most important qualities to the job. It's easy to get bogged down by all of the things that these people are not. Most important, of course, they're not you. But their names wouldn't be on your lists if they weren't also special to you and your family in some important ways.

At this point, it doesn't hurt to just take a moment to feel blessed in having the family and friends that you do. The family that you have, and the one that you have created, is what you can count on to keep your children safe and happy as they grow up, even if you're not there.

If no one left on the list is the obvious choice, pick the person you feel most loves your children and that your children most love. Don't judge the answers you get; just listen to what your heart tells you to do.

EXAMPLE: One couple I know spent years trying to decide which of their sisters to choose as guardians. All of their sisters were lovely, but all of them had some drawbacks. One lived too far away. One had three kids already. One had children already grown and out of the house. One was struggling financially. So they did nothing and had no estate plan at all.

One day, as they were about to go to the hospital for the birth of their third child, the wife's best friend, whom she'd known since high school, arrived to take their other two children to stay at her house. The children hugged their parents goodbye and clambered into her car. As the friend backed out of the driveway, with the children waving away and grinning tearfully, the parents both knew suddenly that the friend, not their sisters, was the right person to name as guardian. After that, writing their wills was easy. (They had the baby first, though.)

After you make your choice, write it down (there's a place to record the names in the Busy Family's Toolkit on the CD) and congratulate yourself. And if you still feel less than certain about your decision, remember that nothing is written in stone. You can always amend your will to change these names as your children get older or as your friends and family's lives change.

If you've gotten this far and still can't figure out who to pick, see "Common Problems and Some Solutions," below, to see whether any of those ideas can help break the logjam. If none of them do, here's my advice: Pick someone anyway. Make yourself pick at least one guardian and get your will done, and resolve to revisit your decision in a year. If the decision is this hard for you, you don't want to place it in the hands of a judge.

Special Concerns for Same-Sex Couples

If you are raising children with a gay partner, the best estate planning strategy is to make sure that you are both the legal parents of your children. That way, if one of you died, the surviving partner would be the remaining legal parent, and there would be no need for a court to get involved or name a guardian. In the states that allow registered domestic partnerships or civil unions (California, Hawaii, Maine, New Jersey, and Vermont), stepparent adoptions (which are much simpler, less expensive, and quicker than regular adoptions) are available for registered couples, making it easier to adopt a partner's child than it used to be. In other states, regular adoption procedures are available, but states vary on their willingness to allow same-sex couples to adopt.

If the second parent can't adopt or just hasn't done it yet, the legal parent should name the second parent as the guardian. Otherwise, if the legal parent dies, the survivor might not get legal custody. In some ways, any stepparent is in this boat, but a member of a same-sex couple is more at a disadvantage in most states, since his or her relationship to the child's parent isn't recognized under state law. But as mentioned, the parent's choice, written is a will, carries a great deal of weight with a judge.

> **RESOURCES**
>
> For more information on gay and lesbian parents and guardianship, see *A Legal Guide for Lesbian & Gay Couples*, by Denis Clifford, Frederick Hertz, and Emily Doskow (Nolo).

Common Problems and Some Solutions

If despite your best efforts, you find yourself really stuck on whom to name as guardian, it might be because you've run into one of the problems listed below. These go beyond the "nobody's perfect" problem. If you've hit one of these, you're probably not being persnickety. Your problem is that, for one reason or another, *nobody* on the list is a likely candidate, or that the person likely to get the job is the person you're least likely to pick. Solving your problem will take some creativity, determination, and flexibility. Read on for some tips that may help.

Your First Choice Is Older Than You Are

Solution: Forget about what could happen in ten years; just pick someone now and reevaluate in five years.

Many parents find it easier to come up with potential guardians if they focus on who could take care of their children in the next three to five years, knowing that they can change their guardian choices as their children, and the nominated guardians, grow older. When children are young, grandparents and other family members are often the best choice. But as children grow up, they become increasingly connected to their own friends and community and don't want to move away from their homes. And grandparents aren't usually the guardians of choice for teenagers. Remember, right now you're choosing someone for the next few years only. When some time has passed, you can reevaluate and make changes.

EXAMPLE: Phillip and Clara have two young sons, aged one and four. They live in Los Angeles. Clara's parents, who are in their mid 60s, are in good health and live in Raleigh, North Carolina, where Clara grew up. Phillip and Clara think that for now, Clara's parents would be the best possible guardians for their boys. They agree to name them as guardians now and to revisit that choice in no longer than ten years, when the boys will be 11 and 14.

Your First Choice Is Not a Good Money Manager

Solution: **Name someone else to handle the finances.**

Sometimes parents hesitate because the person they like best is not a good money manager. That problem is easily fixed. You can name someone else to manage your children's money and leave the guardian with only the job of making sure your child grows up well cared for and as happy as possible. (Naming a financial guardian is covered in Chapter 3.)

> **EXAMPLE:** Bernard's sister, Carol, has a terrific relationship with his two daughters, aged six and eight. Carol would make a wonderful guardian—except that Bernard is concerned that Carol wouldn't do a good job managing the money he'd be leaving for the girls (she'd spend it all on treats). So he names Carol as the personal guardian for his girls but puts his sister-in-law, Jasmine, in charge of their money. Jasmine's job would be to manage the money, letting Carol focus on providing a loving home for the girls.

You Don't Like Your First Choice's Spouse

Solution: **Name the individual, not the couple.**

What if only one person in a couple is your choice for guardian? Just name the person you want—not both of them—as guardians. That way, if the couple divorced, your kids would stay with the person you feel closest to.

EXAMPLE: John wants to nominate his sister Shirley as the guardian of his three children but would not want Shirley's husband, David, to ever have legal responsibility over them. The solution to this to name only Shirley, not David, as a guardian. As long as Shirley and David are married, the children would live with both of them, but if Shirley and David were to divorce (as John secretly hopes that they will), the children would stay with Shirley.

Of course, if you are certain that you wouldn't want your child to live with the spouse you don't like, then you'll have to name someone else entirely. If you object to the person that strongly, it's going to a deal-breaker.

Your First Choice Lives Far Away

Solution: Name a temporary guardian in addition to a permanent guardian.

With today's scattered families, it's common to want to name a guardian who lives in another state or even another country. There's no requirement that a guardian live where you live, but as part of the court proceeding in which a judge appoints a child's guardian, a nonresident may have to post a bond (a sum of money or an insurance policy) as insurance that they will faithfully perform their duties as a guardian. In addition, an out-of-state guardian would have to ask the court in the county where the probate proceeding is occurring to move the guardianship proceeding to the state where they live. This means more hassle (and more lawyer's fees), but it is something that courts will approve if it makes sense for the child.

For international guardianship, the procedure varies from state to state. But as a general matter, guardians living in another country will have to ask the court to name them as temporary guardians here, and then ask a court in their home country to appoint them as permanent guardians there.

If you want to name someone far away as a guardian, it also makes sense to nominate someone local who could serve as a temporary guardian. This person could take care of your children until your permanent guardians could get to them. You can do this by stating in your will that you want the named person to serve as a temporary guardian, if that's ever necessary.

EXAMPLE: Vinod and his wife Bindu, who live in Ohio, want to nominate their parents, who live in India, as the guardians of their three children. In their wills they nominate their parents as guardians and also nominate their best friend and neighbor, Katherine, to serve as a temporary guardian should that be necessary.

You Have Children From Previous Marriages

Solution: Focus on the needs of your children. You may end up naming different guardians for different children.

Blended families are common these days, making guardianship choices even more complicated. Some parents name different guardians for the children of different marriages. Others make a plan that would keep all the children together. The only rule of thumb is to do what's right for the children. Remember that guardianship doesn't come into play at all if a child has a surviving parent, and that's more likely when their parents are not living or traveling together.

EXAMPLE: Lisa and Harold both have children from previous marriages. Lisa has a teenage daughter, Claire, who lives with her and sees her father in the summer. Harold has a teenage son, Jonathan, who lives part time with his mother and part time at Harold's house. Lisa and Harold also have two young children, Richard and William, together.

In her will, Lisa nominates her best friend Leslie as guardian for Claire, in case Claire's father couldn't, or wouldn't, take custody of her. She also nominates her sister-in-law, Ruth, as the guardian for her little ones, Richard and William, in case she and Harold die before the boys grow up. She doesn't name a guardian for Jonathan, who is her stepson.

In his will, Harold nominates his brother, Henry, as a back-up guardian for Jonathan. He also nominates his sister, Ruth, as the guardian of Richard and William.

You Don't Want Your Ex-Spouse to Get Custody

Solution: Name a guardian and state in your will why your ex shouldn't get custody.

If you're divorced, you may be unhappy with the idea that should you die first, your ex-spouse would get custody of your children. That's the reality, though, with just a few exceptions. A court could deny custody to a parent who has abandoned or abused children. Or a parent could agree that another person, such as a stepfather, could serve as the child's guardian. But such situations are rare.

If you really don't want your ex-spouse to take custody of your children, you can explain why in your will. Wills, however, are public documents after someone dies, so you might not want to put such personal information in yours. One alternative is to write a letter stating your reasons for not wanting your former spouse to get custody. Include court records, police reports, or any other evidence of your ex's unsuitability as a custodial parent. Give that letter to your first choice for a guardian, to be used in the case of a court proceeding as evidence of your wishes.

EXAMPLE: Charles is a divorced father of a five-year-old son, Ethan. He has sole custody of Ethan and is not on good terms with Claudia, his ex-wife, who he believes has a drug abuse problem. In his will, he nominates his sister, Amelia, and his brother, John, as guardians for Ethan. He states in his will that it is his wish that Claudia not be granted custody of Ethan. He also writes a letter stating his reasons. In it, he details his experience with Claudia's drug abuse. He gives the letter to Amelia and John and tells them to use it (in court) if Claudia tries to get custody of Ethan.

Your Family Doesn't Like Your Choices

Solution: Explain your wishes in writing.

You may want to make a guardian choice that you're pretty sure your family wouldn't support. Whether it is because you've adopted a different religion or moved to a different part of the country, or because you are gay and your family doesn't approve of your partner or friends, this can be a painful part of estate planning.

Your first loyalty is to your children, and you should always make the choices that you think will serve them best. You should also know that a court challenge to your choice of guardian is very unlikely—and very unlikely to succeed. A family member who wanted to overturn your choice of guardian would have to go to probate court and prove to the judge that there was a very good reason—say, a child abuse conviction—to set your choice aside.

Still, for the sake of your children, it's best to prevent conflict and preserve family relations as best you can. One way to address possible family dissent is to simply discuss the issue with those family members you most fear will be disappointed. You might be favorably surprised at their reaction.

Whether or not your fears turn out to be well-grounded, it's good to leave a written explanation of your choices. It can calm tension later, when family members have different recollections of what you told them. And if necessary (again, this is very unlikely), it could be used in court. After all, if there ever is an argument, you won't be around to defend your choices.

Of course, deciding what to do is a personal choice, which depends on your family members and your relationship with them. Doing nothing is a common choice—the prospect of a family fight over guardianship can be paralyzing. But making some effort now may save a lot of heartache later.

Here are a few different techniques to consider:

Write a letter to family members. In the letter, explain why you feel that your choices are best for your children and ask your family to respect your wishes. Make sure to label the letter so that it's clear it's to be opened only in the event of your death. Keep it with your estate planning documents.

Write a letter to the person you've chosen to be the guardian. Explain in detail all the reasons why you don't want certain people in your family to be granted guardianship and give this letter to your guardian, to be used as evidence in a court proceeding in the future, if necessary.

Put your reasons in the will itself. You can go into as much detail as you want, but keep in mind that your will is going to be a public document upon your death.

EXAMPLE: John and his registered domestic partner, Gary, have a three-year-old daughter, Chandler. They have both adopted her. John and Gary feel that if it were ever necessary, Chandler should be raised by Gary's sister Joan and her husband. But John believes that his mother, Victoria, would fight his wishes in court if she didn't get custody of Chandler, whom she adores.

He feels that Victoria would only be hurt by any discussion of this issue now (and, of course, he expects to live long past Chandler's 18th birthday). So he decides to write a letter to his mother, to be opened only if he and Gary die before Chandler is an adult, explaining that he and Gary love Victoria very much but want Chandler to grow up in a household on the west coast, with other children, in a community that is more supportive of gay parents than the one that Victoria lives in.

RESOURCES

More information on gay and lesbian parents and guardianship.
See *A Legal Guide for Lesbian & Gay Couples,* by Denis Clifford, Frederick
Hertz, and Emily Doskow (Nolo).

SEEK ADVICE

Get help now if you fear a challenge later. If you think that
there is a serious possibility that someone in your family would contest your
guardianship nominations, you should see an estate planning attorney, who
can help you design an estate plan to withstand such a challenge.

You Worry That Your Children Won't Like Your Choices

Solution: Talk it over with them.

If you are worried that your children won't like your nominations
for guardians, you might want to discuss it with them, especially if
they're already in their teens. Even younger children, though, often
have opinions about this and sometimes are comforted in knowing
who would take care of them if parents couldn't. Also, children 14 or
older (12 in some states) may ask the court for a different guardian
from the one nominated by their parents. The judge will take their
wishes into account along with other factors.

After You've Chosen a Guardian: Talking It Over

After you've narrowed your list down to two (or even better, three)
people, you need to ask them whether they'd be willing to serve as
your children's guardians. (You don't, of course, need to tell your
other friends and family that you haven't chosen them, unless you
feel that will help them accept your choices. Boundless candor is not
always the best policy.)

It's really important to have this conversation with the people you've chosen. You might find out that they've already agreed to serve as guardians for other friends or family and feel uncomfortable taking on another potential obligation. You might learn that your guardian is going to need more financial assistance to make a blended family work than you thought. It's true that you're going to provide money for your children's needs, but if the guardian needs a bigger house or a car, you'll need to do some planning to make sure that you can provide that for them also. (Life insurance can help, and I'll talk more about that in Chapter 7.)

How should you bring this up? Try being direct. Find a quiet moment and mention that you are doing estate planning. Say that you would like to know if they'd be willing to be named as a guardian in your will. Let them know that you thought long and hard about it and made the choice because you love them, or that your children do. But also make it clear that you understand that this is a big responsibility, even though the odds of it happening are, thankfully, low. Make it clear that "no" is an acceptable answer, and find out whether there's anything that you can do to make the prospect of being your child's guardian easier. Maybe you could take out more life insurance or arrange things so that if they became guardians, they could live in your house until your children are mature.

You'll probably find out that they haven't done any estate planning themselves (most people haven't). You might find out that they've been meaning to ask you to be the guardian of their children. Or you might find out that there are reasons why you shouldn't use them as guardians, reasons that you would never have known if you hadn't had the conversation. Truthfully, there's no downside to this chat. You really have to have it if you're going to feel comfortable with the decision you've made. And if you're not comfortable with the conversation, maybe you need to reconsider your choice.

TIP

Hit the road. Before you finalize your choice, think about taking a short vacation with your first-choice candidates, even if it's just a quick trip to the beach or lake. I can't tell you how many times clients have chosen guardians during our initial interview, then called the next week and changed their minds after a disastrous weekend together. Sometimes, when you're really trying hard to visualize someone else as your child's guardian, you'll see things about their parenting style that you just didn't notice before.

Giving Guardians Some Written Guidance

Now that you've chosen your guardians and discussed this with them, you might also want to write a letter to them, explaining why you chose them and what you hope they will be able to do for your children. This letter is to be opened only in the event that someday they're appointed (which means that you're not there to discuss things). Sometimes the very thought of this letter brings parents to tears. If you feel that way, don't write it. But if writing down your thoughts and feelings will make you feel good and provide some guidance to the guardians, now's a good time to do it.

Here are the kind of things you might want to include:

Your reasons for choosing them. If you have chosen a friend, not a family member, explain why. This section is important if you think that your family might contest your choice. But it's always a good thing to let your family know that you thought long and hard about this and to explain why you decided as you did.

What you want them to know about your kids. Here's where you can write down any special instructions on how you want your children raised, such as lessons in certain things, travel to certain places, and important family rituals or connections.

Your feelings about education. If you have strong feelings about how your children should be educated, let the guardians know. Some parents want their children to go to certain high schools or colleges; others have strong feelings about graduate schools or other professional programs.

Your feelings about religious education or faith. If it is important to you that your children maintain their ties to a particular church or congregation, rabbi, or minister, let the guardian know. If you want your children to celebrate certain life events, like confirmation or bar or bat mitzvah, that's important to share.

Your wishes concerning your children's relationships with extended family. If you want your children to visit Ireland to see their grandparents every year, let the guardian know. If there are certain family members that you do not want your children to spend time with, let them know that, too.

Your wishes concerning ethical values. If you want your children to learn certain ethical values or to continue your family's commitment to certain social goals such as environmental activism or contributing to charities, write that down here. You might also want to write a letter to your children about these values, so they know what was important to you and why.

Whew! You've just done the hardest part of estate planning for parents. You should feel extra good right now. After working through guardianship, the rest is just details and logistics. There's nothing so emotionally charged left for you to do. But don't stop, either. You still need to make some important choices about how your children's inheritance will be managed for them. And until you put your choices down in a legally witnessed will, they don't count in a court of law. So carry on.

■

Get Organized

....

What you'll do here:

☐ Make a Family Inventory.

....

Y
ou picked guardians first because that's such an important, and difficult, step. The next step in making your estate plan is to understand what you own, and the best way to do that is to complete the "Family Inventory" in your Busy Family's Toolkit on the CD. Making an inventory will prompt you to gather all the information you'll need to make your estate plan. That's the good news. The bad news is that doing it is really boring.

There's no way around that, but you don't have to do the whole job at once. You can tackle one category at a time until you're done. If organizing isn't your thing, that's okay. Just take one stack out of the hall closet at a time, figure out what you've got in there, and throw it back in when you're done, if that's what you need to do to get through this process. If you're anything like most of my estate planning clients, you already have almost all of the information you need in one place or another, but you've never organized it one place before.

Even though creating a family inventory is dry as dirt, it makes a big difference. It gives you a picture (for many families the first one ever) of what you have to leave to your children. If you're not happy with what the inventory tells you, you can do something about it—for example, by buying more life insurance (see Chapter 7 for information on that).

Without some organizing up front, it can take a family months, or even years, to understand what a deceased person left behind. You don't want your loved ones to sort through your messy desk, your unopened mail, and all of the boxes in the garage just to figure out where your safe deposit box is or where your bank accounts, retirement assets, and life insurance policies are. An inventory will make it a lot easier to settle your affairs and transfer assets to the right people.

Worse, you wouldn't want your family to miss inheriting assets just because no one knew that they existed. It happens all the time. One executor I knew discovered that his sister owned hundreds of shares of a valuable stock only because he opened her mail and found a mysterious dividend check. She had never told him, or her children, or her estate planning lawyer, about that investment. Another man learned that he had inherited stock from a brother only when the Pennsylvania Treasury Department's Bureau of Unclaimed Property sent him a letter, years after his brother had died.

If finding and organizing all of this information sounds daunting, remember that you are going to do it in small pieces, and that much of this information isn't likely to change often. Once you've gathered your records, you won't have to do much of the legwork again. After the initial inventory, all you have to do is take an annual look at the list to see what, if anything, has changed. And think how organized you'll feel!

Your family inventory is really just a list of:

- what you own
- where it is
- how you own it
- how much it is worth, and
- how to access it electronically.

As you start identifying and valuing your assets, don't be overly concerned with exact financial figures. The inventory isn't meant to substitute for a financial plan. The reason you want to try to place a value on your assets is so that you can determine, in a general way, how much would be left behind for your children should you die unexpectedly.

You also need to know what kinds of things you own so that you can be sure your estate plan properly deals with them all. Most people don't know this, but wills control only some of the assets that you own. If you think of your family assets like a big pie, your will controls who gets a big slice; but your retirement plans, life insurance policies, property, and certain bank and brokerage accounts will pass outside of your will. You need to make a complete inventory and make sure that you deal with everything on the list. That's what the rest of this book is for—but to get the best use of it, you need to do some homework first.

The rest of this chapter goes through the major categories of common assets. To help you keep track of things, start filling in the family inventory on the CD.

How Assets Pass to Their New Owners

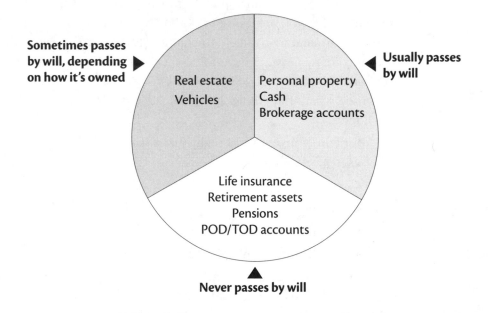

RESOURCES

Organizing help. For a terrific book on how to organize all of your records for your family, see *Get It Together: Organize Your Records So Your Family Won't Have To,* by Melanie Cullen with Shae Irving (Nolo). It comes with a helpful CD-ROM, so all the forms and worksheets are easy to fill in and modify. If you want to use software, try *Personal RecordKeeper* (Nolo).

Cash

Your first task as the family detective is to list each bank account your family has, where it is located, whose name is on the statement, and how much is in it. For the inventory, count checking accounts, savings accounts, and CDs (certificates of deposit) as cash assets. Also write down any electronic access information, such as an account name and password—without that critical information, it could be difficult for your family to gain access to the accounts.

Here's an example:

Cash

What Is It?	Where Is It?	Who Owns It?	How Much Is It Worth?	Electronic Access?
Checking Account # 1234-6789	Bank of America; Duane Street branch	John and Mary	$12,000	PIN # is 1234-5678
Savings Account # 1234-6789-123	First State Bank	John	$1,000	PW=Family ID=1234-789
Certificate of Deposit # 123-567-890002 3-year term; matures 2009	Citibank	Mary	$25,000	No
Checking Account #1002-34009	Employees Credit Union	John and Mary	$10,000	No

College Savings Plans and Custodial Accounts for Children

In addition to bank accounts that you have for your family, you or others might have opened bank accounts or other investments for the benefit of your children. Include these in your inventory—after all, one of the main reasons you're doing estate planning is to make sure that you know your children will have enough, financially, should you pass away. In the unlikely event that you died while they were still young, these assets would be part of the legacy you'd be leaving them.

Custodial Accounts

Bank and investment accounts that hold money or stock for the benefit of children are called custodial accounts. The child is the account owner, but until the child reaches a certain age (21 in most states), an adult must serve as the custodian for the account, and is the only person legally able to invest and spend the assets in the account. A child who has reached the required age can spend the money without adult supervision or control.

You can tell by looking at a brokerage or bank statement whether or not an account is custodial. Custodial accounts usually say something like "for the benefit of" your child's name or have the abbreviation "UTMA" or "UGMA" after the child's name. (Those letters stand for the laws that authorize custodial accounts, the Uniform Transfers to Minors Act and the Uniform Gifts to Minors Act.) For example, at the top of the statement you'll see the name of the account's custodian.

College Savings Plans

If you've opened up a tax-deferred college savings plan for your children, list it. Like the custodial accounts, this is money that could be used for the benefit of your children.

Two kinds of tax-advantaged plans are available today. The first, called "529 plans" after the section of the tax code that creates them, are investment accounts that allow families to save for their children's college and graduate school expenses. Every state offers a 529 college savings plan, and you can invest in any state's plan, even if you don't live there. (The states' plans differ in investment options and performance, and some states offer in-state residents a tax advantage if they invest in their home state's plan.) These state-operated investment plans give families a way to save money for college that's free of federal tax.

Some states also offer a 529 prepaid tuition plan. These plans let parents lock in future tuition at certain (mostly public) colleges and universities at present prices.

The second tax-advantaged saving plan is the Coverdell Education Savings Account, which used to be called the Education IRA. These are savings accounts that are limited to $2,000 annual contributions.

College Savings Plans and Custodial Accounts

What Is It?	Where Is It?	Who Owns It?	How Much Is It Worth?	Electronic Access?
Scholars Choice College Savings Plan Billy's: Account No. 12-56 Jane's: Account No. 13-56	Colorado plan; statements in file cabinet of desk	Mary is custodian; John is backup custodian for both	Billy's: $8,500 Jane's: $3,500	Yes: User ID = DoeFamily Password = elvisrocks
Charles Schwab, CUTMA Account, No. 34-999 For benefit of Jane	Account statements in financial binder, left bookcase	John is custodian	$10,000	Yes: PIN #: 567-888JKL
Edward Jones, Coverdell Education Savings Account, No. 23-888 For benefit of Billy	Account statements In financial binder, left bookcase	Mary is owner	$4,000	No

Safe Deposit Box

If you have a safe deposit box, make sure to write down where it is and (very important) where the key is. If you are going to store your important estate planning documents in the box, know that in some states, it can take several weeks after someone dies for the executor or trustee to gain access to the box. (In Chapter 10, I'll discuss options for storing your estate plan in more-accessible ways.)

Safe Deposit Box

What Is It?	Where Is It?	Who Owns It?	How Much Is It Worth?	Electronic Access?
Safe Deposit Box, Number 56B-CDF-990	Bank of the North, 5567 North Oak Street Branch	Mary		No. Key is the small brown one, in envelope in top desk drawer marked "Safe Deposit Box."

Real Estate

If you own a home, you need to understand how you own it—legally, the way you hold title to it. It is important because if you own your home with others, the form of title affects who would own it upon your death.

If you don't know how you own your house, you are not alone. Most people don't remember what they put on the forms when they were signing that six-inch stack of papers to get their home loan. To find out, look for the grant deed that transferred legal ownership of your house from the former owner to you.

If you can't find your grant deed, don't panic—just read the tips below. If you have something called a Deed of Trust in that file folder that you have from when you bought the house, that's *not* what you're looking for. That's what gives your lender the legal right to repossess your property if you don't pay off the loan, but it isn't the piece of paper that states that you own the house in the first place.

How to Find the Deed to Your House

If you can't find a copy of your grant deed, ordering a duplicate is easy. Once the deed has been recorded–that is, filed with the county land records office after the house sale is completed—it is a public record. You can order yours from the county in which your home

How to Order the Deed to Your House

Call your county's land records office. It is often called the county recorder's office, land registry office, or county clerk's office. Or visit its website to find out how much it costs to order a grant deed. There is usually a certain fee for a one-page document and an additional, smaller fee for each additional page.

Send a letter requesting your deed, along with a check for the required amount and a self-addressed stamped envelope, to the county office. The letter can be as simple as this one.

County Recorder's Office
Green County
1234 Government Lane
Green City, CA 12345

Dear County Recorder:

Please send me a copy of the grant deed for my property, located at 1234 Elm Street, Green City. Enclosed is a check for $_____, along with a self-addressed stamped envelope. Feel free to call me at _____ or email me at _____ if you have any questions.

Thanks,

Property Owner

Property Owner
1234 Elm Street
Green City, CA 12345

is located for a nominal fee, usually about $10. In some counties you can even order it online and have it mailed to your home. Title companies can also order deeds for you but often charge a bit more than the county does for the service.

Forms of Ownership

Once you've found your deed, take a look and see what it says about how you own the property. Here are examples of what you might find:

- John, as his sole and separate property (SP)
- John and Mary, husband and wife, as joint tenants (JTWROS)
- John and Mary, husband and wife, as community property (CP)
- John and Mary, husband and wife, as community property with right of survivorship (CPWROS)
- John and Mary, husband and wife, tenancy by the entirety (TBE)
- John, Mary, and Jane, as tenants in common (TIC)

Each way of owning property describes how the people on the deed share ownership and affects what happens if one of them dies.

Separate property. If you own property as your separate property, that usually means that the property is yours to give away at death to whomever you want. I say "usually," though, because in community property states—Arizona, California, Idaho, Nevada, New Mexico, Washington, and Wisconsin—a spouse may own a share of such property, even though only the other spouse's name is on the deed itself, if wages earned during the marriage were used to pay off the mortgage or make improvements on the property. (See Chapter 4 for a more in-depth discussion on how spouses can own property and leave it to each other.)

Joint tenancy. The most common way for couples to own property is as joint tenants. This means that they each own an equal share in the property and that when one owner dies, the survivor owns the entire property by what lawyers call "right of survivorship." The surviving joint tenant gets the property automatically; property owned in this way can't be left to others by a will or a trust. The reason that this form of property ownership is so common is that it allows the surviving joint tenants to avoid the probate process altogether. (See Chapter 5 for a discussion of probate and why people like to avoid it.)

Community property. In community property states, married couples (and registered domestic partners as well) can own property as community property. That means that they each own a half-interest in the property. Unlike joint tenants, owners can pass their halves by will or trust upon their death.

Community property with right of survivorship. Just to make this even more complicated, certain states—currently Arizona, California, Nevada, Texas, and Wisconsin—allow married couples (and in California, registered domestic partners) to own property as community property with right of survivorship. When couples own property this way, when one of them dies, the survivor automatically owns the entire property by right of survivorship, without a probate proceeding.

Tenancy by the entirety. In about half the states, married couples (and in some states, registered domestic partners) can own property as tenants by the entirety. Like joint tenancy, this form of ownership means that the surviving spouse or partner owns the entire property, without a probate proceeding.

Tenancy in common. You might also see a deed in which multiple owners are listed as tenants in common, especially in cities where apartments are being sold to multiple owners in the hope of eventually converting each unit into a separate condominium. Tenants in common can divide their interests in unequal ways (one person can own 80% and another 20%, for example), and each owner can pass his or her interest by will or trust at death.

Real Estate

What Is It?	Where Is It?	Who Owns It?	How Much Is It Worth?	Electronic Access?
House	1234 Redbud Lane, Center City	John and Mary, husband and wife, as joint tenants	$275,000 market value; $150,000 equity	No
Condo	1126 Union Court, #23	John, Mary, and Jane, as tenants in common	$155,000 market value; $56,000 equity	Mortgage account can be accessed: PW = mollycat ID = 1234-90

RESOURCES

More about property. For more information on property owner-ship (and just about every other estate planning topic), see *Plan Your Estate*, by Denis Clifford and Cora Jordan (Nolo).

More information on domestic partners' rights. For information about your state, see *A Legal Guide for Lesbian & Gay Couples*, by Denis Clifford, Frederick Hertz, and Emily Doskow (Nolo).

Investments, Retirement and Otherwise

To make sense of the investments your family has, start by gathering all the statements that you can find into one pile. Then sort that big messy pile into two neat piles: one for your IRAs, Roth IRAs, 401(k)s, 403(b)s, and annuities, and one for all the rest.

The first pile is made up of statements for all of your retirement accounts. The reason you're sorting them into a separate pile is that these accounts all have *beneficiaries* you've named on record with the plan administrator or investment manager. Those beneficiaries will receive any money left in those plans when you die; you won't deal with retirement assets in your will or trust. If you want to leave those assets to a new person, you have to update those beneficiary designations with the companies themselves, using a Change of

Beneficiary Form that they'll send to you. (We'll talk more about this in Chapter 6.)

The second pile is made up of all of your other investments. These might be brokerage accounts that contain stocks, bonds, or mutual funds; or mutual funds that you've bought directly from a company such as Franklin-Templeton or American Century Funds; or stocks that you purchased directly from certain large publicly traded companies, such as Johnson & Johnson or IBM. Depending on how you own these investment accounts, you may leave them through your will or trust, or they may pass automatically to a joint owner. If you and your spouse, for example, own them as joint tenants, the surviving spouse will automatically own the whole account when the first spouse dies. Or you can fill out a form with the company that holds the accounts to make them "payable on death" or "transfer on death" accounts, which means that they will pass to the person you designated, just like the retirement accounts with designated beneficiaries. (You'll learn more about that in Chapter 8.)

Now take a closer look at the account statements in each pile. Look at the person to whom the statement is addressed to see who is listed as the legal owner of the account. If it is addressed to both members of a couple, they're both on record as the legal owners. If only one member is listed, that person is the legal owner of the account. In community property states, though, your spouse might own some of the account, too, even if it's just in your name. (This can get complicated, but for right now the most important thing is to add up everything that you own as a family, to see what your kids would have if both you and your spouse weren't around.)

Next, see if you can find any abbreviations after the names on the statement. If you have designated a beneficiary for these accounts, it will usually be listed at the top of the statement, some-times with an abbreviation "FBO," which stands for "for the benefit of." If you haven't named a beneficiary for an investment, look for "JTWROS" along with the account owners' names at the top of the statement. That means that you own the account as a joint tenant with the listed person. If you own an account separately, you'll see just one name at the top of the account. You can leave it to someone in a will or a trust, unless you live in a community property state, in which case your spouse will most likely own some share of the account.

Investments

What Is It?	Where Is It?	Who Owns It?	How Much Is It Worth?	Electronic Access?
Retirement Investments				
Roth IRA, Number 123-456	Vanguard	Mary	$45,000	PIN = 23-45
401(k)	TIAA-CREF	John	$62,000	PW = parkingspace2
Nonretirement Investments				
Franklin-Templeton Investments, Tax-Free Bond Fund, Account No. 123-999	Franklin-Templeton	John and Mary, JTWROS	$10,000	None
Charles Schwab One Account, No. 23-456	Schwab	John	$23,000	User ID = HWong PW = sailboats

RESOURCES

More on avoiding probate. For a great guide to payable-on-death accounts, transfer-on-death accounts, and other ways to avoid probate, read *8 Ways to Avoid Probate*, by Mary Randolph (Nolo).

Life Insurance

Life insurance is an important part of family estate planning. Often, the proceeds from a policy are the major source of immediate cash for a surviving spouse or young children. You'll need to find out which policies you own, how much each policy would pay upon the death of the insured person, and who the beneficiaries are for each policy. During your lifetime the value of your life insurance is minimal—what we care about here is the amount it would pay out if you were to die.

The first place to look for insurance coverage is at work. Your employer might offer you group life insurance that will pay a set amount or some multiple of your annual salary. Sometimes, you can buy additional coverage at a reasonable cost through such group plans. So, you need to know what your employer offers as basic coverage, as well as whether you've purchased any additional coverage. It may be hard to get the name of the actual insurer from your Human Resources department, especially at big companies where the plan providers can change often. But all group life insurance policies are identified by a group certificate number, so for your inventory get that, and the amount of the policy, if you can't get anything else. Your employer might also have purchased an accidental death policy, which will pay your family an additional amount if you die as a result of an accident. List the group certificate number for this policy as well.

If you've bought additional life insurance outside of work, you should have your insurance policy filed somewhere. That's where you need to look to find out what kind of life insurance policy you've bought, how much it will pay upon your death, and whom you named as beneficiaries. Each policy you own has a policy number. If you can't find the policy, you can look on your premium bill (it may come monthly, quarterly, or annually) to find the policy number. Once you've found the policy number, you can either go online or give the insurance company a call to find out what you've got. If you can't find your policy or a current bill but know the name of the insurance company, call and see if you can find out what your policy is, what it covers, and what the policy number is.

Sometimes credit card companies or banks offer small, free insurance policies to card or account holders. For example, you might get a $10,000 accidental death policy when you open up a checking account or take out a new credit card. Write these down on your inventory as well.

In the course of your research, you may discover that your policies have the wrong beneficiaries. You might, for example, have forgotten to change these designations after getting divorced or having a new child. That's easy to fix. In Chapter 7, you'll learn how to change your policy's beneficiary designations and whom you should be naming.

Pensions

You might have a pension plan through a company or a government agency you worked for or a union you belong to. These are sometimes referred to as defined-benefit plans. Some pensions will end at your death, but others may make payments, called survivor benefits, to a surviving spouse or children. Find out how much it would be worth to your family if you died (sometimes there is no value to the surviving family members; it depends on the pension plan). And find out how your family should contact the plan administrator.

Annuities

Annuities are similar to life insurance policies. You sign a contract with a company in which you agree to deposit a certain amount of money, and they agree to pay that money back to you over a certain period. Sometimes these policies pay a benefit to survivors, and sometimes not; check with the issuing company to find out whether an annuity has survivor benefits or not.

Life Insurance, Pensions, and Annuities

What Is It?	Where Is It?	Who Owns It?	How Much Is It Worth?	Electronic Access?
West-Coast Insurance Co., 20-year term life policy (expires 2020)	File cabinet of desk	Mary, Policy Number 123-4567 Beneficiaries: John, primary; children, secondary	$500,000	No
West-Coast Insurance Co., 20-year term life policy (expires 2020)	File cabinet of desk	John, Policy Number 123-4559 Beneficiaries: Mary, primary; children, secondary	$500,000	No
Planters Beneficial Life, Universal Life Insurance	Safe deposit box at Bank of the North	Mary, Policy ABX-009-YHHT Beneficiaries: John, primary; children, secondary	$500,000	No
Large Co., Group Life Policy	Check with H.R. department at work	John, Group Certificate Number 234-56	$900,000	No
Large Co., Group Accidental Death and Dismemberment Policy	Check with H.R. department at work	John, Group Certificate Number 234-222	$1,000,000	No
State Employee Pension Plan	Information is available at the state website	Mary No survivor benefits. Employee ID No. 345-56-7889	Depends on when Mary retires	Yes: User ID = MDoe Password = sailboats
Planters Beneficial Life	Policy is in safe deposit box at Bank of the North	John Beneficiary: Mary Doe Fixed Annuity Contract, No. 2307777	$25,000	No

Government Benefits

If you or your spouse would be entitled to any veterans benefits, disability benefits, or other government benefit, make note of them here.

Automobiles and Personal Property

The cars you own, as well as your furniture, jewelry, and other personal items, are likely to change over time more than anything else on the inventory. So list only those items that are either worth a significant amount or that mean a lot to you.

Moving On

Now that you've figured out what you've got, on to your real task: understanding how to manage all of it for your children and how to make sure that they'll inherit enough to grow up happy and safe. The worst's over. Take a break and recover from your detective work. Make a cup of tea. From now on, you'll be making decisions about the people you love and how best to take care of them. Everything you've done so far will help make your decisions well-informed and your estate plan comprehensive. Good work.

Family Inventory

What Is It?	Where Is It?	Who Owns It?	How Much Is It Worth?	Electronic Access?
Cash				
Checking Accounts				
Checking Account #1234-6789	Bank of America; Duane Street branch	John and Mary	$12,000	PIN # = 1234-5678 PW = Family ID = 1234-789
Savings Accounts				
Savings Account #1234-6789-123	First State Bank	John	$1,000	No
Certificates of Deposit (CDs)				
Certificate of Deposit #123-567-890002 3-year term; matures 2009	Citibank	Mary	$25,000	No
Safe Deposit Boxes				
College Savings Plans and Custodial Accounts				
Custodial Accounts				
Charles Schwab, CUTMA Account, No. 34-999 For benefit of Jane	Account statements in financial binder, left bookcase	John is custodian	$10,000	Yes: PIN #: 567-888JKL
529 Investment Plans				
Scholars Choice College Savings Plan Billy's: Account No. 12-56 Jane's: Account No. 13-56	Colorado plan; statements in file cabinet of desk	Mary is custodian; John is backup custodian for both	Billy's: $8,500 Jane's: $3,500	Yes: User ID = DoeFamily Password = elvisrocks
Coverdell Education Savings Accounts				
Edward Jones, Coverdell Education Savings Account, No. 23-888 For benefit of Billy	Account statements in financial binder, left bookcase	Mary is owner	$4,000	No

What Is It?	Where Is It?	Who Owns It?	How Much Is It Worth?	Electronic Access?
Real Estate				
House				
House	1234 Redbud Lane, Center City	John and Mary, husband and wife, as joint tenants	$275,000 market value; $150,000 equity	No
Condo	1126 Union Court, #23	John, Mary, and Jane, as tenants in common	$155,000 market value; $56,000 equity.	Mortgage account can be accessed: PW = mollycat ID = 1234-90
Other Investments				
Brokerage Accounts				
Charles Schwab One Account, No. 23-456	Schwab	John	$23,000	User ID = HWong PW = sailboats
Mutual Funds				
Franklin-Templeton Investments, Tax-Free Bond Fund, Account No. 123-999	Franklin-Templeton	John and Mary, JTWROS	$10,000	None
Partnerships				
Stock Options				
Retirement Investments				
Roth IRA, Number 123-456	Vanguard	Mary	$45,000	PIN = 23-45
401(k)	TIAA-CREF	John	$62,000	PW = parkingspace2
Automobiles				
Minivan	home	Mary & John	$10,000	No
Camry	home	John	$4,500	No

What Is It?	Where Is It?	Who Owns It?	How Much Is It Worth?	Electronic Access?
Personal Property				
Jewelry				
wedding ring	home	Mary	$3,000	No
Furniture				
miscellaneous	home	Mary & John	$8,000	No
Other Collectibles				
Art				
Life Insurance, Pensions, and Annuities				
West-Coast Insurance Co., 20-year term life policy (expires 2020)	File cabinet of desk	Mary, Policy Number 123-4567 Beneficiaries: John, primary; children, secondary	$500,000	No
West-Coast Insurance Co., 20-year term life policy (expires 2020)	File cabinet of desk	John, Policy No. 123-4559 Beneficiaries: Mary, primary; children, secondary	$500,000	No
Planters Beneficial Life, Universal Life Insurance	Safe deposit box at Bank of the North	Mary, Policy ABX-000-YIIII7 Beneficiaries: John, primary; children, secondary	$500,000	No
Large Company, Group Life Policy	Check with H.R. department at work	John, Group Certificate No. 234-56	$900,000	No
State Employee Pension Plan	Information is available at the state website	Mary No survivor benefits. Employee ID No. 345-56-7889	Depends on when Mary retires	Yes: User ID = MDoe Password = sailboats

What Is It?	Where Is It?	Who Owns It?	How Much Is It Worth?	Electronic Access?
Planters Beneficial Life	Policy is in safe deposit box at Bank of the North	John Beneficiary: Mary Doe Fixed Annuity Contract, No. 2307777	$25,000	No

Choose Someone to Manage Your Children's Money

What you'll do here:

☐ Choose someone to manage any money your children inherit.

☐ Pick a method (custodial account or trust) to manage these assets.

☐ Name a "property guardian" as a backup measure.

Your next step is to choose someone who would be responsible for safeguarding, investing, and spending any money your children inherited from you while they were still young. Choosing someone who could raise your children if you couldn't is hard (really hard). But picking someone to manage the money and property that they might inherit shouldn't be nearly such a puzzle. This person's job is to make good investment decisions and spend that money for your children's benefit. You don't need to find the next Warren Buffett. You just need to choose someone who is diligent, responsible, honest, and thoughtful about money management.

In most cases, of course, parents leave their money and property to each other. Their children inherit only if both parents pass away. So although money management is an issue you need to consider when making your estate plan, the odds are that the person you choose won't ever have anything to do. Even if you or the other parent died while the children were young, the surviving parent would simply inherit the deceased parent's assets and carry on, taking care of themselves and the family.

For many people, the personal guardian and the money manager are going to be the same person. That's a great choice for many families. After all, you do both jobs now: get the kids ready for school *and* manage the family's money to make sure that there's enough to take care of their needs.

But if the person that you want to name as your children's guardian isn't good with money—you fear he or she would squander your children's money on ponies or be overwhelmed by the task of responsibly investing and spending their money—you can pick someone else. You should pick someone who will invest your children's money even more carefully than they would invest their own. You should trust this person to exercise judgment about how that money should be spent and be fair to all of your children. And if you pick someone other than the guardian to manage the money, you'll need to make sure that the two of them will be able to work together well.

The Busy Family's Toolkit on the CD contains a worksheet for recording your choices. For now, jot down the people who first come to mind. You can make your final decision when you've picked a method for managing the money your children might inherit.

In addition to picking the right people to manage your children's money, you'll need to pick the right way for them to manage that money. You have two good choices, both of which are discussed in detail below:

- **a trust**, which allows you to select a trustee to manage money and other property for whatever purposes you specify, until a child turns whatever age you choose. You can create trusts for each of your children or one "pot trust" for all of them, or

- **a custodial account**, which allows someone you've named to manage a child's money and property, until that child turns 18 (in a few states), 21 (in most states), or up to 25 (in a few states).

Once you've picked a person and a method, you can pull your plan together by filling out the Inheritance Planner worksheet. A sample is below; a blank form is in the Busy Family's Toolkit. You can fill it out as you work through this chapter, not all at once. When you've completed this chapter, you'll use what you've decided to create a simple will in Chapter 4. The key to getting your estate plan done without stressing yourself out, after all, is to pace yourself and do it little by little.

Inheritance Planner

How	Who	For How Long
Custodial Accounts	Custodians: 1. _____ 2. _____ 3. _____	Custodial account should end at age _____ . [If your state allows you to choose.]

Trusts	Trustees:
	1. _Jennifer Smith_
	2. _Joseph Doe_
	3. _____
	and
	Cotrustees:
	_____
	and
	_____
		☐ Separate trusts for each child.
		   Trust ends when each child is _____.
		OR
		☑ Pot trust
		   Trust ends when youngest child is _27_.
		   Interim Distributions:
		   _10%_ at age _24_
		   _____ at age _____
		   _____ at age _____

Both methods, custodianships and trusts, make sense for some families and some situations. In many ways, they're similar. Each of them provides a way to manage a child's property until they're adults; each allows the money manager to take reasonable compensation for the work of taking care of your children's money. But they differ significantly in several key respects, including:

- how long management lasts, and
- how much flexibility they offer.

To know which one is better for your family, you need to understand how each one works. It's a little like shopping for the latest digital wonder device. You might not need all the bells and whistles that the most expensive model offers. Sometimes, a simpler, lower-cost option has everything you need. The important thing is to understand which features are essential and which ones you can live without.

Before you can make that decision, you need a rough idea of what your children might inherit from you. Many of my clients are surprised at just how much their kids would inherit when they add up life insurance, home equity, retirement, and cash. You might be happy to have your 25-year-old inherit $50,000 outright, but it would be a completely different situation if the amount were $500,000. The more money your children stand to inherit should you die, the older you're likely to want them to be before it falls into their hands.

Look back at the family inventory you made in Chapter 2 and fill in the big-ticket numbers here, to get an estimate. All you need is an approximation, so round things off to the nearest $10,000 or so.

How Much Could Your Kids Inherit?

(List your assets and liabilities to the nearest $10,000)

Assets	Value	Liabilities	Net Value
Your house	$275,000	$75,000 mortgage	$150,000
Condo	$155,000	$100,000 mortgage	$55,000
Cash (savings, checking, CDs)	$45,000	$5,000 credit card debt	$45,000
Nonretirement investments (brokerage accounts, mutual funds, etc.)	$30,000		$30,000
Options	none		none
Retirement accounts	$100,000		$100,000
Life insurance policies (what they would pay out if you died)	$2 million		$2 million
Personal property (cars, jewelry, etc.)	$20,000		$20,000
Annuities	none		none
Business assets (what you think they could be sold for)	none		none
		Total Net Worth	**$2.4 million**

Planning for Children With Special Needs

If you have a child who may never be able to manage and invest funds without help, you face a special challenge, and the estate planning techniques discussed in the rest of this chapter will not accomplish your goals. If your child relies on government benefits for essential services and support, inheriting money could jeopardize eligibility for those services, at least until the funds are spent. For most families, the key fear is losing Medicaid coverage, because their special needs child may never have a job that provides health care insurance.

Medicaid and some other programs are available only to those who can't pay for such care themselves. This means that leaving a disabled child money directly can cause the opposite result than that intended by a well-meaning parent.

To leave your child money to live a meaningful and comfortable life, without losing the support of government programs, you will probably want to create a "special needs trust," also called a "supplemental needs trust." This type of trust can be structured so that a trustee manages a child's property for that child's entire lifetime. Because legally the child does not own or control the trust assets, those assets won't cause your child to be disqualified from receiving essential government benefits.

For lots of helpful information on this topic, read *Special Needs Trusts: Protect Your Child's Financial Future*, by Stephen Elias (Nolo).

Custodial Accounts

If you don't mind the idea of your children getting complete control over their inheritance at a relatively young age—18 to 25, depending on where you live—then you may want to use a custodianship. It's definitely the simplest method and can work well for some families.

Setting Up a Custodial Account

A custodial account is usually a bank or brokerage account that is opened in the name of a minor child. You can open an account like this at any time. If it is part of your estate plan, it would be opened after your death by the person you'll name as your executor. (See Chapter 4.) The person in charge of the account is called its custodian.

Setting up a custodial account is easy. All you need to do is to state in your will or trust that any money your child inherits from you should go into a custodial account and name a custodian to manage that account. If there are other kinds of assets—real estate, for example—the custodian can manage them, too.

There must be a separate custodianship for each child; you can't pool your assets for the benefit of them all. Each child's account can be used to benefit that child only. If one child had extraordinary medical expenses, for example, the custodian couldn't dip into his brother's or sister's custodial account to pay those bills. This can be a significant drawback to using custodianships.

State law (the Uniform Transfers to Minors Act) determines how the account must be managed, what the money can be spent on, and when the account must end. Every state except South Carolina and Vermont has adopted this law so that people can easily leave property to children.

In most states, the custodianship ends when a child reaches the age of 21, though some states allow you to choose to terminate the account when a child reaches any age between 18 and 25. (You can see how your state handles this by looking at the table below.) A custodial account is really a simple trust created for a child's benefit, with standard terms, that you can use and everyone else understands. For example, banks and other financial institutions know exactly when the property in a custodial account must be distributed to a child, and what the money can and can't be used for. And opening a custodial account at most banks and other financial institutions is free.

Using Custodial Accounts for Your Children's Assets

Pros	Cons
Easy to set up	You can't restrict the use of the money for any specific purpose, such as education.
Low or no cost	
One size fits all	An account can't be set up to benefit multiple children.
Familiar to all financial institutions and easy for a custodian to manage	An account must end when state law says it must end. After a custodial account ends, the money must be turned over to the child with no strings attached.

When a Child Receives Property Held by a Custodian

State	Minor Receives Property at:	But You Can Change Age to:	State	Minor Receives Property at:	But You Can Change Age to:
Alabama	21		Missouri	21	
Alaska	18	Up to 25	Montana	21	
Arizona	21		Nebraska	21	
Arkansas	18	Up to 21	Nevada	18	Up to 25
California	18	Up to 25	New Hampshire	21	
Colorado	21		New Jersey	18	Up to 21
Connecticut	21		New Mexico	21	
Delaware	21		New York	21	
Dist. of Col.	18	Up to 21	North Carolina	18	Up to 21
Florida	21		North Dakota	21	
Georgia	21		Ohio	18	Up to 21
Hawaii	21		Oklahoma	18	Up to 21
Idaho	21		Oregon	21	Up to 25
Illinois	21		Pennsylvania	21	Up to 25
Indiana	21		Rhode Island	21	
Iowa	21		South Dakota	18	
Kansas	21		Tennessee	21	Up to 25
Kentucky	18		Texas	21	
Maine	18	Up to 21	Utah	21	
Maryland	21		Virginia	18	Up to 21
Massachusetts	21		Washington	21	
Michigan	18	Up to 21	West Virginia	21	
Minnesota	21		Wisconsin	21	
Mississippi	21		Wyoming	21	

What a Custodian Does

Once money or property is placed into a custodial account, the assets belong to the minor child but are controlled by the custodian. The custodian is required to manage the money prudently—no investments in risky start-ups or penny stocks would be legal. The custodian may spend the money for the use and benefit of the child. For example, money in a custodial account could be used to pay for housing, food, education, a computer that a child would use for school, summer camp, extracurricular activities, a car, or a trip to Italy.

Custodians must keep good records on how they spend the funds in custodial accounts, and they have to file tax returns on behalf of the minors who benefit from them. (Income from a custodial account must be reported on the child's tax return and is taxed at the child's rate.) There is no court supervision of custodians, and there are no specific restrictions on how a custodian must manage the assets, other than carefully and for the benefit of the child. The custodian has a legal duty to be scrupulously honest, keep custodial funds separate from personal funds, and act in the child's best interest. But no one is looking over the custodian's shoulder to make sure that this happens.

Naming a Custodian

Picking a custodian for your children's custodial account is often simple. You're looking for the person you know who is the most trustworthy and the best able to manage money. If that's the same person you've already chosen to serve as your guardian, that's fine. But it's also fine to name a different person for the money job—if the two get along.

When Custodial Accounts Make Sense

Easy to understand and set up, inexpensive or even free, custodial accounts can be great in certain circumstances.

A custodial account's main virtue, simplicity, is also its main vice. Custodial accounts are terrific for people leaving small gifts to nephews and nieces but are not usually a great choice for most parents. There are two main reasons.

First, most parents don't want their children to inherit everything at 18 or 21. But unless you're in one of the few states that let you delay termination until your child turns 25, you're stuck with the younger age.

Second, most parents would like to provide for more flexibility in how their children's money should be managed. They might want to provide more money for one child than another, to require a money manager to give money for certain life events such as graduation or marriage, or to allow money to be used for certain things but not for others (for college, but not for tattoo school). For this kind of control and flexibility, you need to create a trust. You can leave instructions for the custodian (please don't spend money for video games), but the final decisions will be in the custodian's hands.

However, if you are leaving behind a modest estate, a custodial account might be a terrific option for your family. It's hard to define "modest"—but for most people it's an amount that a custodian could reasonably be expected to spend before a child turns 21. For example, if college costs $25,000 per year, leaving $100,000 in a custodial account might be just the ticket. That way, after four years of college, the money would be spent, so you wouldn't have to worry about a child's ability (or inability) to manage it at 21.

Custodial accounts cost nothing to set up, although some institutions require a minimum investment. If your will leaves money to your children and states that it should be held in an UTMA custodianship, then your executor, working with the named custodian, would open custodial accounts for the children after your death. Banks and financial institutions would help them fill out the proper forms. Once the accounts were opened, your child's money would be managed by the trusted adult you chose and could be spent on anything your children needed. A custodian is legally entitled to compensation for managing an account, but in most families, custodians choose not to take any pay for the job.

EXAMPLE: Emory, who is eight years old, inherited $500,000 when her parents passed away. In their wills, they had named her Aunt Agatha as the custodian of an account, to be established for the benefit of Emory, that would hold their entire estate. They had also requested that a custodial account for Emory be created to hold the proceeds from their $250,000 life insurance policy. Until Emory is 21, her aunt can use that money to provide for Emory's health, education, and welfare. Agatha put most of the money into a custodial brokerage account, where it is invested in a balanced portfolio. The rest is in a custodial bank account that she uses to pay for Emory's daily needs.

When Emory turns 21, whatever money is left in both accounts will be entirely hers to invest and spend as she chooses. This worries her Aunt Agatha, who feels that Emory should finish college and make a start in life before taking over the management and investment of her inheritance. But there's nothing Agatha can really do when Emory turns 21, except to offer to keep managing the money for Emory and hope she takes her up on the offer.

Creating a Custodial Account

If you want to establish a custodial account for your children, you can do it in your will. You name the person whom you want to serve as the custodian of the account and state what assets would go you into the account at your death. If your state allows it, you can also choose the age at which the custodianship ends. It also makes sense to name an alternate custodian, just in case your first choice is unable or unwilling to serve as custodian later.

Trusts

If you want to leave a significant amount of money to your children, pick someone to manage it until the children are older than 21, and be able to give the person in charge both clear instructions and flexibility, then a trust is the way to go.

A trust is a legal entity that holds assets (money and other property) for the benefit of certain people, called the beneficiaries—your children, in this case. Trust assets are managed by a trustee you choose, who follows the rules you've laid out.

When you use a trust, you identify which assets should go into the trust, pick the trustees you want to manage these assets, and decide how old your children should be before they inherit the assets outright.

As an estate planning tool, trusts are flexible. For example, you could specify that your children not get control over all the money you've left them until they're 35. Or, if you want to ensure that the money will be used only for certain things (a down payment on a house, but not a sailboat trip around the world), you could impose restrictions on the use of the money. You can make one trust for all your children or a separate trust for each one.

You can set up a trust for your children by making certain decisions about all these issues and writing them down in your will (see Chapter 4) or in your living trust (see Chapter 5). Either way, the trust created for your children will function in exactly the same way.

It's important to remember that the children's trusts you may create as part of your estate plan won't exist unless both you and your spouse die, and only then if your children are younger than the age you've chosen for ending the trust. Until then, you are in charge of the money and can use it for whatever you want to.

EXAMPLE: Lee and Marjorie, a couple with four young children, create a will leaving their estate to their children in trust until the youngest child turns 30. Their will says that if they die after their youngest turns 30, the children each receive an equal share, outright. When Lee dies, the youngest child is 28. When Marjorie dies, the youngest child is 42. All of the children receive 25% of the estate left by their parents. A trust is never established at all.

> ### Things to Decide When You Create a Trust
>
> - Whom to name as trustee, the person who will manage the property.
> - Whether to establish a separate trust for each of your children or to pool the money for the benefit of all of them.
> - What the trustee can and can't use the money for.
> - When the trust will end, giving your children money outright.

What Trustees Do

Before you choose a trustee, it's good to get an idea of what trustees do and what they should be good at. For once, a legal term is very descriptive—you should pick someone you trust completely. Your trustee will be in charge of managing your children's money. Unless someone challenges their performance and goes to court, they'll be doing it without court supervision, possibly for many years.

Trustees must manage trust assets carefully, competently, and honestly. If the trust has more than one beneficiary, the trustee must be impartial. Treating beneficiaries impartially doesn't mean treating them all equally. If you created a pooled trust for all of your children, for example, it wouldn't be proper or legal for the trustee to send one of your children to Harvard because she liked that child best, but to tell the other three that there was no money left for their college expenses at all. But if one child needed an expensive medical procedure, and one of the trust's purposes is to provide funds for the beneficiaries' medical care, it would be proper for a trustee to use trust assets to take care of that child, even though it would leave less money for the other children.

The trustee's job is to administer the trust solely in the interest of the beneficiaries. That means that trustees are not allowed to use trust assets to benefit themselves or for any non-trust purpose. It wouldn't be okay, for instance, for trustees to purchase trust assets (such as your house) for their own use, use trust money to buy things (such as a new car) for themselves, or invest trust funds in their own companies. It would also be improper for a trustee to live rent-free in a house owned by the trust while serving as trustee, unless the trust said that was okay.

Trustees don't need to be stellar money managers, just prudent and diligent ones. In states that have adopted a law called the Uniform Prudent Investor Act (40 states have), trustees must, unless a trust says otherwise, invest and manage trust funds by looking at the portfolio as a whole, rather than each investment in isolation. They must also balance risk against return given a particular trust's purpose and beneficiaries. That means that a trustee of a children's trust could invest money in a stock that is growing quickly (like Google) but not paying dividends yet, as long as other investments provided more long-term stability. In some states that haven't adopted this law, there are more restrictions on investments. For example, trustees may be limited to certain kinds of conservative investments, such as bonds, instead of growth stocks.

To help sort out which investments to make and how to comply with state and federal law, trustees are allowed to hire people to help them make good decisions and get good advice. For example, it's common for a trustee to consult a lawyer at the beginning of the process and to get an investment adviser to help figure out how to invest the trust funds properly. Trustees may use trust assets to pay these experts reasonable fees.

The trustee must file annual trust tax returns with both the state and the federal government, reporting the income and expenses of the trust in each tax year. Trust taxation has slightly different rules from those for personal income taxes, mostly around the issues of how to tax capital gains earned by the trust. That's why many trustees hire accountants with expertise in trust accounting, called fiduciary accounting, to prepare these returns.

The trustee must also provide periodic accountings to the beneficiaries, detailing how the money has been invested and spent. How often the trustee must give these reports depends on the trust and on state law. Depending on the terms of the trust itself and state law, these reports can be informal (such as a copy of the annual tax return or a simple spreadsheet showing income, expenses, gains, and losses) or formal, prepared by an accountant following the standard rules of fiduciary accounting. In either case, a trustee who understands what is required should be able to do them or to hire an accountant for the job.

Trustees are entitled to reasonable compensation for the work that they do to manage trust assets. It can be a big job to manage a trust if there are complex assets to manage or if the trust lasts for many years. In many families, however, trustees, like custodians, often choose not to be paid.

Naming a Trustee

Picking a trustee for your children's trust, like picking a custodian, is usually pretty straightforward. Pick the person you know who is the most trustworthy and the best able to manage money. Again, if that's the same person you've already chosen to serve as the children's guardian, that's fine if the person can do both jobs well. (You do both jobs, after all.)

Many families, however, select different people to serve as guardian and trustee because one person is better at managing money or because they want to keep both sides of the family involved with the ongoing care of the children. It's fine to name a different person for the money job, as long as the guardian and the trustee can work together and communicate well.

> **EXAMPLE:** Diego and his wife, Carmen, nominated Grace, Carmen's sister, as guardian of their two children. They named Clara, Diego's sister, as trustee. They did this because Clara is a certified public accountant and because they wanted both families to be involved in their children's lives if a guardianship were ever necessary. Clara and Grace get along well and live in the same state.
>
> If Diego and Carmen die, Grace, the guardian, will have to request that Clara transfer trust funds to her on a periodic

basis to cover everyday living expenses for the children. If Clara doesn't agree with Grace's wish to spend trust funds on a certain private school or a new computer system, she'll have the final word because she has the power of the purse. Unless Grace, or someone else concerned about the welfare of the children, is willing to bring a lawsuit against Clara for violating the terms of the trust or her duties as trustee, there won't be much she can do about it.

More Than One Trustee

You can name two people to serve together as trustees. This is called serving as cotrustees. Usually, families who do this are trying to make sure that both sides of a family stay involved with the children. There's no legal barrier to naming cotrustees, but there are some personal and logistical factors to consider before you do so.

Because cotrustees share the legal responsibility for the trust decisions they make, such as how to invest and spend funds, the general rule is that any power shared by cotrustees is shared equally—they must both agree on all actions.

If cotrustees can't agree, important trust decisions might not get made quickly—or at all. At the least, you could be looking at all sorts of bad feelings. At the worst, if cotrustees just can't work it out, and there are no provisions in the trust to resolve conflicts, one cotrustee would have to go to court to settle the dispute. Because one of the main reasons families create trusts is to avoid court meddling in family affairs—and because lawsuits eat up huge amounts of money and escalate family fights—nobody wants this to happen.

On the logistical side, even if both cotrustees agree, getting double signatures on all documents can be a hassle if they don't live in the same place. You can give cotrustees the power to delegate certain actions to each other, but if a trust says nothing about this issue, the general rule (all cotrustees must authorize everything) applies. One client of mine resigned as a cotrustee so that her brother, the other trustee, could take care of trust business without needing her to cosign documents.

SEEK ADVICE

Avoiding future trouble. If you think that there are issues in your family that might create conflict over who should serve as trustee or if you own a family business or other complicated assets that require a trustee with specific expertise, consult an estate planning attorney before choosing a trustee.

Siblings

Here's one bad idea I hear fairly often: naming one child to be the trustee for younger siblings. It sounds like a nice idea, especially when there's a large age difference between your oldest and your youngest child, but it can be a terrible source of conflict. Even if the trustee is scrupulous about being fair to younger brothers and sisters and is careful to never benefit at their expense, it's a difficult position. If a younger brother or sister asks for money to fund a pet project or purchase a house or a business, and the trustee says no, there are bound to be bad feelings.

Grandparents

Another thing you need to think about is the age of the trustee. Naming a 75-year-old grandmother as trustee if you have a three-year old isn't a terrific idea. Just do the math: If the trust is set up to last until that child turns 30, your trustee would be 102 when it ends. Your trustee is aging, right along with your kids. If you really don't have another first choice, go ahead and name your parent, but make sure that you also name a second choice who's in your generation, just in case. That way, if your trustee is unable or unwilling to continue managing the trust, the next person on the list can step forward for the job.

Professional Trustees

Some parents just can't come up with anyone who they think is capable of, or interested in, managing money. If that describes your situation, consider choosing a professional money manager to serve as a sole trustee or as a cotrustee with a family member. Professional trustees are also known as trust officers and private fiduciaries. They work in the trust department of banks, at financial institutions, or independently. It is most common to name a professional trustee in wealthy families. But it can be a great idea for any family if the remaining family members would not be up to the task of managing a portfolio or there is likely to be conflict among family members over managing and spending funds.

Professional trust officers charge for their services, usually a percentage of the assets under their management. These fees vary greatly from place to place and depend upon the size of the trust being managed. As a rule of thumb, they charge an annual fee of between .75% and 1.25% of the assets being managed. One large trust company charges .80% of the first $750,000; .70% of the next $750,000; .60% of the next $750,000; and .50% on all assets over $2.5 million. The larger the trust fund, the less the fee is as a percentage of the total trust, but the greater the dollar amount of trustee compensation. If, for example, you hired this company to manage a $1 million fund, the annual fee would be $7,500.

Some professional trustees will not accept the job unless trust assets are large, and all of them have a minimum trust amount that's required before they'll take on the job. The required minimum investment varies greatly: Merrill Lynch, for example, currently requires a minimum investment of $1 million; Fidelity requires at least $300,000; and Edward Jones won't handle anything less than $250,000.

There are a few disadvantages to using a professional trustee. Sometimes families feel that a professional trustee isn't personally enough involved with the trust or the beneficiaries to make the sensitive decisions that the job can require. For example, what if a trustee must decide whether or not a child is mature enough to use trust assets to buy a house, go to graduate school, or have a fancy wedding? Another drawback is that a trustee's financial institution, such as the local bank, might be purchased by another bank, and then another. Before long, a family is dealing with a trust department in another city, with people that none of them know.

Don't dismiss the possibility of hiring a professional trustee out of hand, though, if you think it might make sense for your family. It might be worth it to have a professional on the job. The money your estate spends in fees might be made up for because the trust investments do better than they would have if a family member were in charge.

Talking to Professional Trustees: What to Ask

✓ What is your investment minimum?

✓ What are your fees?

✓ How are your fees calculated?

✓ If my trust were approximately $500,000, what would the annual fee be at your institution?

✓ What are the annual returns on trust investments over the last five years?

✓ How do these returns compare with industry performance over the same five-year period?

✓ How do you communicate with beneficiaries?

✓ What do your annual statements look like?

✓ Who would manage my trust account?

✓ What is your firm's investment portfolio like for trust accounts?

✓ Would it be possible to speak with three trust customers about their experience with your trust services?

It isn't hard to find a professional fiduciary. Many financial service companies and banks have trust officers who manage trusts for families. Your local bank, too, may offer such services. To find a private fiduciary, look for a professional fiduciary's association online or in the phone book. Each association has its own rules and qualifications, but that's the best way to find qualified professionals in your area.

If you decide that you do want to name an institution to serve as a professional trustee, make sure to check with someone there before you do so. They may have specific wording that they want you to use in your will or trust. They might even want to review a draft of your will or trust before they agree to offer their services. (They want to make sure that you're giving the trustee the right powers to enable them to do the job properly and offering them sufficient protection against lawsuits if they do their job honestly.) If you want to name a specific branch of a national company, you can do so, but I always worry about being that specific—if the branch closes down or moves, you don't want your family left guessing about what to do. It's often better to name an institution and then appoint a family member, called a "trust protector," to select the particular branch to deal with.

One Trust or Many?

Once you've selected a trustee, your next job is to decide how your trust should be structured. Really, the decision boils down to whether you want to pool your family's money for the mutual benefit of your children or create separate trusts for each child.

If your children are less than five years apart in age, pooling their funds usually makes the most sense. That way, the trustee can spend more money on the children who need it the most, while remaining fair, of course, to the others. For example, one child might need expensive orthotics for his shoes; a couple of years later, his sister might need to go to a special school. A family pot trust would work well here because the trustee would have access to all of the family's money and could distribute it as needed to the children. When the trust ends, all the children get an equal share of what's left in the pot.

Most parents, after all, do the same thing. They don't set apart identical sums to be spent on each child no matter what (even if some kids would think that perfectly fair). You use what you've got to give your children what they need, and when they're grown and you're no longer around, they will share whatever's left.

> **EXAMPLE:** Sasha and her husband, Jonah, establish a family pot trust in their wills for their three girls, aged three, five, and seven. In the very unlikely event that Sasha and Jonah die before all of the girls are at least 28, all of Sasha and Jonah's assets will go into a trust for the girls. They choose Jonah's sister, Marjorie, to serve as the trustee.
>
> The trust states that money is to be used for anything that the girls need for their health, education, support, and maintenance. At 23, or upon graduation from college, whichever happens first, each girl is to receive a gift of $20,000 from the trust. When the youngest daughter turns 28, the trust will end, and each girl will receive a third of what remains in the trust. That means that, if the trust were created when the children were young, the oldest girl would have to wait until she was 32 to receive her share. It also means that everyone would share what was left after college expenses had been paid out. If one child went to an expensive private college, one had gone to a state school, and one hadn't gone to college at all, they'd still all share what was left equally.

If your children are more than five years apart in age, or you want their ultimate inheritance to be affected by which college they attend, it makes sense to create separate trusts for each of them. It makes the trustee's job of being fair to all a bit simpler when it comes to the big-ticket items.

If everyone starts out with the same amount of money when the trust is funded, older trust beneficiaries can go off to college— usually the single biggest trust expense—knowing exactly what their budget is. Meanwhile, younger children are assured that their older siblings aren't using more than their fair share.

With separate trusts, a child who goes to an expensive private school will have less trust money after graduation than a sibling who chooses a state school or doesn't go to college at all. Some parents feel that a pricey degree is a reasonable investment of the money and don't worry about the child leaving school with less cash on hand.

Separate trusts make it easier to terminate each trust, too. If a trust ends when a child reaches 30, for example, and each child is to receive an equal share of the trust assets at that point, older beneficiaries aren't going to get their share until the youngest turns 30, because the trustee won't be able to calculate equal shares until then.

> **EXAMPLE:** Kevin and Sharon have four children, aged two, six, ten, and 14. Because there's such a big age difference between their youngest and oldest, they decide to establish a trust that, if it's ever created, will divide into four equal shares. Each share will be managed by the same trustee, and the money in each can be used for health, education, maintenance, and support of that child. When a child reaches the age of 23, that child will receive $20,000 from his or her share. At 25, each child will receive 25% of what's left in his or her share, so that they can get some practice managing and investing money.
>
> When each child turns 28, that child will receive the balance of his or her share. That means that, if the trust were created when the children were young, the oldest son would get his money when his littlest sister was only 16. It also means that each child began with an equal share, but that what they have left after college will be affected by where they choose to go. If one daughter went to an expensive private college, for example, she'd have less in her trust upon graduation than her sister who chose a state school or received a full scholarship.

How Long Should Your Trust Last?

It's not easy deciding when a children's trust should end. I've noticed that parents of toddlers tend to get dreamy-eyed when imaging the future financial acumen of their now-tiny children. Parents of teenagers, though, don't always have such a rosy view. Sometimes they even ask me if they can arrange it so that their kids *never* get their hands on the money.

I tell my clients to think back to when they were old enough to responsibly handle money. For some parents, that's around 30, for others it's earlier, and for some it's later. Whatever the right age is for your family, that's probably when your trust should end.

And trusts should end. Sooner or later, unless your children have special needs or serious credit problems, they will want to manage and spend their money for themselves. I've heard several adult beneficiaries of trusts complain about having to wait too long to gain control of their inheritances. In one case, a woman wanted to buy a house after she graduated from college but had no access to the trust funds from her deceased father's insurance policy until she was 30. Of course, trust terms can give trustees discretion about such things, but her trust did not. Think about when you'd like your children to begin managing and investing their money. That would be the age of your youngest child when the trust terminates, if you use a pot trust, or the age of each child if you use separate trusts for each child.

> **WARNING**
>
> **Special needs require special trusts.** Again, if you have a child with special needs who depends upon government assistance that is based on financial eligibility, will simply never be able to independently manage money, or both, you will probably need a special needs trust. See "Planning for Children With Special Needs," above.

Giving Out Money Before the Trust Ends

Once you've figured out when your trust should end, you should look backward to college and see if you want to make any interim distributions to your children. In other words, do you want the trustee to give your child a chunk of money at a certain age, or at a certain milestone, while keeping the rest in trust? Money that goes directly to the children would be under their control. Money that stays in trust is still available for their needs but remains under the trustee's control. The purpose of an interim distribution is to give your children practice in managing money themselves, without turning everything over to them. You can even structure it so that no money is paid out to older kids until you're sure there's enough to get the younger ones through college.

If you give a child 25% of the trust money at the age of 25, for example, and that child immediately loses it all in a bad investment or spends it on a fabulous three-year sailing trip, the other 75% of their inheritance is still being safely managed by the trustee you selected.

EXAMPLE: Nareet and her partner Sarah have two children, aged seven and nine. Their current net worth, including life insurance proceeds, is $1.5 million. They decide that their children's trust will be a pot trust, because the children are so close in age. They also decide that by their early 30s, their children will be as financially trustworthy as they're ever going to be. Here's how they decide to distribute the trust over time:

Age of Youngest Child	Trust Distribution	Why Do It This Way?
23 or graduates from college, whichever happens first	Each child gets $20,000.	No money is distributed from the trust until the youngest finishes college. That way, the trustee can be sure that college expenses will be paid for first.
27	Each child gets 10% of the trust assets.	The other 90% of the trust assets are still being managed by the trustee for the benefit of the children. The children get to practice managing their 10%.
32	Each child gets half of what's left in the trust.	The trust ends, and each child manages her own money independently.

How Much Should You Control a Trust From Beyond the Grave?

Even though trusts offer you almost unlimited ability to restrict the use of the trust assets or direct investments, should you? Even if it would mean a lot to you for your daughter to pursue a graduate degree in chemistry at your state university, would it be a good idea to *require* that she do it as a condition of receiving her inheritance? Even if you're sure that a certain stock is going to be a long-term winner, should you *require* a trustee to invest in it?

Put bluntly, no. It's always a terrific idea to communicate your hopes for your children, either directly or in a letter that you can write to them to be opened only upon your death. You can even write a letter to their guardian or to the trustee of your family trust describing your hopes and dreams for your kids or their money. But inserting specific conditions in your trust can mean trouble for those who have to live by its terms. There's simply no way to know what the world will be like 20 or 30 years from now. What if your child has an incredible talent for cooking, not chemistry? What if that dream stock tanks? If your trust is restrictive, and it no longer makes sense for a trustee to follow its directives, the trustee will have to go to court to change the trust's terms. This is expensive and time-consuming, and it might not even work.

A trustee's job is to exercise judgment and discretion. Let your trustee do it. Your trust can give the trustee freedom to give money to your children for a wedding, to buy a house, or to start a business. But let the trustee decide whether any of those things is a good idea for a particular child at a particular time.

> **TIP**
>
> **There are limits on your power.** You're not allowed to require certain things in a trust or a will, because they would be considered against public policy. You couldn't, for example, make a distribution to your son on the condition that he get divorced or take away money if he gets married.

Your Backup Plan: Appoint a Property Guardian

Even though you've chosen a custodianship or a trust for your children's potential inheritance, as a backup you also need to name someone (in your will) to serve as a "property guardian" for your children's property. A property guardian manages any property that your children might own after your death that somehow isn't part of a children's trust or placed in a custodial account.

The odds of your children owning property like this are quite low—right now, you are planning to leave them all of your property in either a trust or a custodial account.

Still, children do sometimes end up owning property of their own. It could be stock given to them by a grandfather or a savings account left to them by an elderly aunt. A more common situation, though, is when a parent or grandparent names a child as a beneficiary for a life insurance policy or IRA but doesn't name a custodian for them on the policy or plan. If the child inherits the money before age 18 and it's worth more than a few thousand dollars, a court must appoint a property guardian to manage the account. Until your children are legal adults, the property guardian can invest and manage the money on their behalf.

Mind you, the problem can be easily avoided by naming a trust that benefits your child as the beneficiary on these plans, or by designating a custodian to manage the asset for your children when you name them as beneficiaries, but it sometimes happens.

Whom should you pick? Most parents nominate the same person they've selected as trustee or custodian to serve as property guardian, should one be necessary. That's a sensible choice, because that's the person you've decided is the best money manager you know. Most parents also name the same person to serve as property guardian for each of their children.

If there's only a small amount of money at stake, less than $10,000 in most states, your executor might be able to avoid a property guardianship. In that case, the executor could appoint a custodian under the Uniform Transfers to Minors Act as long as the will didn't forbid this. The custodian would manage the property for a child until age 18. But if the property is worth more than about $10,000, a probate court must approve the transfer, in most states.

A property guardian is always accountable to the court that made the appointment. While the specifics vary a bit from state to state, as a general rule the property guardian must do a thorough inventory of a child's assets, submit it to the court, and seek court approval for any significant action, such as selling real estate. A property guardian must keep complete, accurate records of each financial transaction affecting the child's property and receipts for all purchases. The property guardian must also file periodic accountings with the court, listing receipts, expenses, income, and assets. The court may ask the guardian to justify some or all expenditures. The guardian must have receipts and other documents available for the court's review, if requested.

Most of the court-required documents are created by lawyers. That means high hourly fees. Property guardians can also apply for reasonable compensation for all the work they're doing. So having a property guardian can be expensive, and the fees are paid from the property your children inherit. For all of these reasons, use a property guardianship only as a backup measure.

> **EXAMPLE:** John, a single father, names his only child, Alexa, who is 12, as the beneficiary of his $500,000 life insurance policy and names his sister, Caroline, as the custodian of the money. Caroline is also the executor of John's will and Alexa's guardian. John dies unexpectedly in a car crash. Caroline establishes a custodial account to hold the life insurance proceeds for Alexa's benefit until she turns 25 (they live in Tennessee, which allows this).
>
> A year after John dies, Alexa inherits a $250,000 IRA from her grandmother, who named her as a beneficiary but didn't name Caroline as the custodian of the account for Alexa's benefit. Caroline must go to court and be appointed Alexa's property guardian so that she can manage the account on her behalf until she turns 18.

Keeping Your Ex Away From the Money

If you are divorced and are concerned about the ability of your ex-spouse to manage your children's money, be extra careful to set up either a trust or custodianship and put someone else in charge of these assets. You'll be happy to know that your ex-spouse doesn't automatically get to be the guardian of your child's property. A judge can name anyone who will do a good job managing a child's money.

You can even request in your will that your ex not be named as your children's property guardian. If you have specific reasons to support your concerns, such as the fact that your ex has never paid required child support payments, you can state these, too. But remember that wills are public documents once you die, and anything in them will be open to public viewing.

Another option, which avoids public scrutiny, is to write a letter detailing your ex's bad behavior and including supporting documentation, and give this letter to your executor. If your ex chooses to contest your wishes after you die, this letter can be introduced as evidence in a court proceeding—and may well be enough to avoid such a hearing altogether.

Make Your Will

....

What you'll do here:

☐ Choose an executor and two alternates.

☐ Complete a simple will.

....

Congratulate yourself. You've already done a lot of the heavy lifting in estate planning. You've had to track down and inventory your property. You've made the difficult decision of whom to nominate as guardians for your children. You've decided on the best way to manage any money that they might inherit and who should do the managing and investing. Now, you'll put all of these decisions together to make a simple will.

Your will is a document, which you sign in the presence of witnesses, that sets out all of the decisions you've already made. But before you're ready to dash to the computer and press "print," there's one more decision left for you to make. In this chapter, you'll choose someone to serve as your executor, also called your personal representative. That person has the job of making sure that all of your wishes are carried out when the time comes.

Why You Need Only a Simple Will

You can do many things in a will, such as forgive outstanding debts owed to you, disinherit family members, and leave money and property to certain people in trusts with varying conditions attached. But here, we'll focus on creating a simple will that, if you're married, leaves all of your property to your spouse. If you're a single parent, you can skip that part and use this will to leave everything to your children.

Here's why. For the vast majority of young families, the simple will in this book will take care of the essentials. It's all you'll need for now. Most parents leave everything they have to each other first; children inherit only if both parents pass away. Most parents leave everything in equal shares to their children—and as an estate planner, I heartily recommend that plan for people concerned about maintaining family harmony and good feelings. And most parents want to make sure that the money they've left behind is to be used for whatever their children need until they're sufficiently mature to manage it for themselves. This simple will accomplishes all of these goals.

What the Will in This Book Does

✓ Leaves all property to your spouse.

✓ If your spouse dies first or at the same time, leaves everything to your children equally.

✓ Names your executor and an alternate.

✓ Names a guardian (and an alternate) for your children.

✓ Sets up a trust or custodial accounts for your children, in case they inherit money from you while they are still young.

Later, when you acquire more assets or if your family relationships become more complicated, you can always revisit and adjust your estate plan. For now, just get it done and cover the basics.

 RESOURCES

If you want more options than this book's will offers, use *Nolo's Simple Will Book*, by Denis Clifford (Nolo), or *Quicken WillMaker Plus* software (Nolo) to create a customized will for you and your family.

WARNING

Don't start yet. Before you actually make the will included with this book, take a moment to read the beginning of Chapter 5, which covers living trusts. If you decide that it makes more sense to create a living trust for your family, you should still fill out the Will Worksheet below, but you'll use those answers to create your trust instead.

What Wills Don't Do

If a will is all you need, you might be wondering why this isn't the last chapter in the book. The truth is that even though a will is the most important legal document you need right now, it is only part of a larger estate plan. You probably own several significant assets— perhaps the most valuable things you own—that aren't governed by your will at all. And you need to take them into account also. (That's what the rest of the book is for.)

Houses, retirement accounts, proceeds from life insurance policies, and even brokerage and bank accounts can all pass to others outside of whatever your will says. If that surprises you, you're not alone. Many people have no idea that their wills don't control what happens to some of their most important assets.

Property You Own With Others

Your will doesn't affect certain property that you own with others, because that property is owned in a way that allows the surviving owners of the property to inherit it automatically when one owner dies. It happens because of the way the property itself is owned, not because of anything written in a will.

The legal term for this automatic inheritance is a "right of survivorship." Joint tenancy is the most common form of property ownership with the right of survivorship, but there are others that function in much the same way. See "When the Surviving Owner Inherits Automatically," below, for a list.

When you made your family inventory in Chapter 2, one of the things you were trying to find out was whether you owned any bank accounts, brokerage accounts, or property in joint tenancy or another form of ownership that carries with it the right of survivorship. If you do, then that property isn't governed by your will; it will go to the surviving owner or owners.

If a couple owns an asset in joint tenancy, for example, then when one of them dies, the other automatically owns the entire thing. For most families, that's terrific, because it is what most families would want to happen, anyway. It also means that there's no need for a probate court proceeding to transfer ownership of the property to the survivor. (There will be a few forms to file, though.)

Couples can own many kinds of property this way. Houses are commonly owned in joint tenancy, as are brokerage accounts, bank accounts, and vehicles. Unmarried partners also use joint tenancy to own property and money together in this way.

You can't override the right of survivorship in your will. If, for example, in your will you leave "everything to my spouse" but own an apartment building in joint tenancy with your sister, she, not your spouse, would own the building after your death.

To find out whether you have any property with a right of survivorship, take a look at your real estate deed and account statements. Look for the abbreviations listed here—usually at the top of the statement, after your names—to decipher what you find. (If your property is owned as community property (CP), separate property (SP), or tenants in common (TIC), it does not carry a right of survivorship, and you can leave your share by will.) Chapter 2 discusses all these forms of ownership.

If you don't own property with a right of survivorship but would like to, you can change the title of your assets to one of the forms listed above. To do that, contact the financial institution holding your money or stock, your state's department of motor vehicles, or a real estate agent or title company.

When the Surviving Owner Inherits Automatically	
Joint Tenancy (JT) (Not called joint tenancy in all states—in Oregon, for example, it's called "Tenancy in Common With Right of Survivorship.")	The most common form of property ownership with a right of survivorship. Two or more people can own property this way; they don't have to be related to one another. Each of their shares must be equal (except in Vermont).
Tenancy by the Entirety (TBE)	About half of the states offer this for married couples and, in some, for registered domestic partners.
Community Property With Right of Survivorship (CPWROS)	Available only in some community property states and only for spouses or registered domestic partners.

Property You've Named Beneficiaries For

Retirement accounts, life insurance policies, and some other kinds of assets also pass outside of your will. On a form provided by the company you name beneficiaries to inherit them and file the form with the company that issued the policy or administers the plan. That beneficiary designation trumps whatever your will says.

> **EXAMPLE:** In your will, you leave everything to your spouse. But you name your sister as the beneficiary for your life insurance policy. (Maybe you forgot to change it when you got married.) When you die, she, not your spouse, will get the money from the insurance.

In Chapters 6, 7, and 8, I'll go into detail on how to integrate your retirement accounts, life insurance policies, and payable-on-death accounts into your estate plan. One of the things you'll do then is to make sure you've named the right people as beneficiaries on those plans. For now, though, you just need to remember that these assets aren't part of what you're giving away in your will.

What Happens If You Don't Make a Will?

It may sound silly to even discuss, in a book like this, what would happen if you don't make a will. After all, you're just about to do it! But people often ask me. I hope knowing the answer motivates you to get it done.

If you don't make a will or any other provisions for distributing your property, your spouse (or registered domestic partner) and possibly your children would inherit your assets. Exactly how much they each would get is governed by state law where you live. The laws for who gets what are called the rules of "intestacy."

As a general rule, only spouses (and registered domestic partners in some states) and blood relatives inherit under state law. Usually, spouses get the largest share. If there are no children, the surviving spouse often gets all the property. If there are surviving children, they usually share with the surviving spouse. More-distant relatives inherit only if there is no surviving spouse or children.

In Virginia, for example, the surviving spouse receives everything if there are no surviving children or if all of the children are also the children of the surviving spouse. If the deceased spouse had children from another marriage, then the surviving spouse gets one-third of the estate and the children get the other two-thirds. It gets more complicated from there.

In the nine community property states (Arizona, California, Idaho, Louisiana, Nevada, New Mexico, Texas, Washington, and Wisconsin), spouses (and registered domestic partners) inherit the community property and a share of the property owned separately by the deceased spouse. The share depends on the number of surviving children or siblings of the deceased spouse.

The states all have their own rules for who would inherit your estate. But wouldn't you rather make up your own?

Not making a will affects more than property. Without a will, a judge would appoint, without any guidance from you, a personal guardian to raise your children and a property guardian to manage their inheritance. A judge will try hard to pick the right people for these jobs, but obviously it's better to leave a list to work from. When you make a will, you state your choice for guardian—a wish the judge would almost certainly honor. Finally, the only way to ensure that your children won't inherit everything you've left them at 18 is to make a will, providing for an alternative to a court-ordered property guardianship or custodianship.

Without a will, your unmarried (and unregistered) partner, close friends, charities, and anyone else you want to take care of upon your death will not receive a penny from you under state law. I know of one committed couple who had lived together for many years. Neither had wanted to marry because they'd both been through several marriages. Sadly, one partner died unexpectedly, leaving behind no will. The survivor inherited nothing and had no protection under state law.

Taking Care of Business: Picking an Executor

Enough background—it's time to get to work. You're finally ready to dig in and get the will done. There's only one job you haven't already filled: someone who will serve as the executor of your estate. The executor's job is to gather all the deceased person's property; pay debts, expenses, and taxes; and distribute what's left to the right people. To do all of this, the executor follows state law and the instructions you've left in your will. And although technically it's not the executor's job, many also make sure that beneficiaries receive all life insurance and retirement plan benefits that they're entitled to.

If your estate plan consists of just a will, your executor will probably need to take the estate through a probate proceeding or hire an attorney to help do it. If your estate plan includes a living trust (see Chapter 5), your estate won't go through probate, and your executor won't have that part of the job.

What Is Probate?

Probate is a process in which a judge makes sure that a deceased person's will is valid, that all property has been inventoried and appraised properly, and that it is distributed to the right people. Probate commonly takes nine months to a year, but the time frame, as well as the expense, depends a lot on where you live. Some states offer quicker, less cumbersome probate procedures than others.

General Things to Consider

Your executor doesn't have to be financial genius. Just pick someone who is organized, trustworthy, and willing to get the job done. Executors can hire experts to help them and can use estate funds to pay them.

It also helps to choose someone who generally gets along with everyone. Settling an estate doesn't always bring out the best in people. Often, in fact, it brings out the worst in them, as otherwise mature people find themselves in heated fights over who should get grandmother's teacup collection or cuckoo clock. A good trustee will be a good mediator—someone who can listen well, crack a joke when humor can help, and stand firm when the will clearly requires it.

Spouses: The Usual Choice

As a rule, spouses get picked first for this job because they are the ones most familiar with all of the assets and because most of the time they'll be transferring the assets to themselves. Transferring assets after the death of one spouse is generally a straightforward process, as long as the executor knows where all of the assets are. (That's partly why I made you do all the boring detective work in Chapter 2.)

You don't, of course, have to name each other as executors. If your spouse would have a difficult time dealing with the details following your death, or if your family has complicated politics, naming a third party, such as a trusted family friend or a bank's trust officer, might be the right thing for you.

More Than One Trustee

Parents of adult children often choose their children to serve as their second and third choice executors. This, of course, raises all sorts of family questions: Will Jane be offended if you pick her brother Robert to serve as executor, and not her? Will Jane and Robert stop speaking to each other if Robert makes a decision as executor that Jane doesn't agree with or thinks is unfair?

Some parents skirt the issue entirely by naming all of their children as coexecutors. But be warned that this means that all of them must agree on every action taken on behalf of the estate and sign off on all of the paperwork, unless the will gives them the authority to act independently.

If your children get along harmoniously, this can work. If they don't get along, or if they live far away from each other, serving as coexecutors can be a logistical nightmare no matter what the will says. It can even, in extreme cases, lead to lawsuits and acrimony. So, it's really a better idea to try to choose one and name the others as alternates, after you've discussed your choices with each beforehand.

Do You Need Someone Close By?

An executor who lives far away might not be the right choice. It might be too expensive or complicated for someone far away to administer an estate, and it will almost certainly require that they spend some time where you lived to put things in order. If you know a responsible person who lives closer, consider naming that person for the job.

Some states, too, have restrictions on out-of-state executors. They might be required to post a bond—a kind of insurance policy to protect the will's beneficiaries—or to appoint someone to serve as their in-state agent (so that the local probate court will have jurisdiction over them). In a few states they just won't qualify, and a judge will have to appoint someone else.

Finding Your Probate Court's Rules

To find out your state's probate rules on out-of-state executors and other matters, start with your county's website. To find it, use this formula: www.co.COUNTY-NAME.XX.us (where XX is your state's two-letter abbreviation). For example, the Santa Clara County, California website is www.co.santa-clara.ca.us, and the Pima County, Arizona website is www.co.pima.az.us. From the website, you should be able to find a link to the local probate court.

Hiring a Professional Executor

If you anticipate leaving a large estate, or if you have fractious relatives, complicated debt issues, or unusual assets, you may want to consider naming a professional executor, such as a bank or trust company. The professional can serve either as the only executor or as a coexecutor with a family member. By doing so, you'll have the advantage of a neutral third party with experience in taking care of an executor's duties and financial expertise that may serve your family well.

A professional executor's fee is usually a percentage of the total estate going through probate, and many professionals handle estates only if they're worth at least a certain amount. An executor's fee for an estate that goes through probate is set by state law and must be approved by the court before it's paid. Family members, though they're entitled to fees for the services they provide, don't always choose to take these fees. (Why? Well, the fees are subject to income tax, but the inheritance they'll get once the estate is settled is not. For most people, waiting to inherit is a better tax move.)

Plan B: Name an Alternate

After you settle on your first choice, you should also come up with one—or even better, two—names of alternate executors, in case your first choice is unable to serve. Just as when you made your first choice, you should pick someone who is good on logistics and details and who could spend the necessary time identifying assets, notifying creditors, dealing with tax returns, and keeping good records. Most important, you should pick someone you trust. Your executor will be carrying out your last wishes, and it's not always an easy task.

Write down your choices on the "My Executors" worksheet in the Busy Family's Toolkit on the CD-ROM.

Now, Talk to Your Choices

No matter whom you pick, it's important to discuss the matter with them before you write your will. It's not fair to surprise someone with such a big responsibility. And someone who doesn't want to serve can always decline to serve when the time comes—and if that's going to happen, it's better to clear it up now. (A client once asked me whether he could name Bill Gates as his executor. I told him he could name anyone he pleased, but that he shouldn't expect a stranger to serve on his behalf.)

Discussing this with your executor now makes sense for him or her, too. Your future executor will probably have questions for you about how you want things handled and where your assets are. Though it can be an awkward discussion to begin, you both might find it a useful one to have.

How to Make Your Will

Finally! Now that you've figured out whom to name as guardians and executors and thought through how to manage money for your children, you're ready to make a simple will. This book contains a form you can use to do just that.

Wills don't have to be (and shouldn't be, really) complicated. Like recipes, they are written in a certain ritualized way and designed to do a specific thing. As long as you get the basic information in them and have them properly signed and witnessed, they'll do what they're supposed to: set out your last wishes clearly and in a legally binding way.

Making It Legal

There are just a few formal requirements for a will to be legal.

- Your will should be typed or printed from a computer. A handwritten will can be valid, but it is much better to type a will so it won't be possible for people to add things to it later.
- You must sign your will in front of at least two witnesses.

Filling in the Blanks

You and your spouse each need a will. To create one, follow the step-by-step directions on the sample worksheet below. A copy for you to use is in the Busy Family's Toolkit. On the left are instructions and explanations; on the right is the will itself, with blanks for you to fill in.

Again, this is a simple will. It leaves everything to your spouse, with your children as alternate beneficiaries. It provides that if your children do inherit while they're still young, the money goes into a trust managed by a person you chose.

It's easiest to print out this worksheet, write in your answers to make a draft, and then transfer your answers to the will form in the Busy Family's Toolkit on the CD. Print out the finished document and sign it using the important formatting and signing instructions provided on the CD, and you'll be done!

Will Worksheet: Example

Will of <u>Mary Ruth Doe</u>	
ARTICLE ONE: IDENTIFICATION OF FAMILY	
Here's where you identify yourself and state where you live. It's also important to make it clear that this is the will that you want people to use, not any previous versions.	I, <u>Mary Ruth Doe</u>, a resident of <u>Green County</u>, state of <u>Missouri,</u> declare this to be my will. I revoke all wills and codicils that I have previously made.
If you are married, identify your spouse here. If you and your partner have registered with your state as domestic partners or gone through a civil union, state that here. (There's language for you to use in the blank worksheet.)	1.1 **Marital Status.** I am married to <u>John Richard Doe.</u> All references in this will to my spouse are to <u>him.</u>
Identify your children (natural born and adopted) and write down their birth dates. It is important to list all of your children, even if you aren't planning on leaving all of them anything, to avoid any claim that you accidentally overlooked a child, who might then be able to claim a share of your estate.	1.2 **Children.** My only living children are <u>Stephanie Ann Doe</u>, born <u>April 11, 2000</u> and <u>Charles John Doe</u>, born <u>December 2, 2003.</u>
ARTICLE TWO: DISPOSITION OF PROPERTY	
These can be gifts of money or of things like your collection of china, jewelry, or books. If you don't have any specific items to give, and many young families don't, you can leave this section out. (But you'll need to renumber the sections below.) It's a good idea to name an alternate beneficiary for specific gifts. If the person that you've named had died before you, the alternate would inherit the gift. The next section of the will takes care of everything	2.1 **Specific Gifts.** I leave the following specific gifts of money or personal property: A. I leave <u>$20,000</u> to the guardian of my children, provided that the guardian is one of the people nominated in this will to serve as guardian.

left over after you've made any specific gifts. If you want to leave any specific gifts—for example, to the guardian of your children or to other people or organizations—you can do that here.

Why leave money to the guardian? You are leaving your children adequate money to take care of their needs, but it would be improper for the guardian to use that money to benefit him- or herself; that's what a separate gift is for.

This section states that everything else you have that's governed by your will, after gifts have been made and taxes and expenses paid, will go to your surviving spouse or partner.

If you are the second to die, then it all goes to your children. Fill in the names of your children here.

If any of your children are under the age you specify here, their money will be held in a Family Pot trust for them. The trustee will invest the money and decide how it will be spent.

If all of your children are at least the age you choose, then they will inherit their share of your estate directly. The money will be theirs to invest and spend.

This is the "god forbid" clause, specifying who should receive your estate if your spouse and your children do not survive you. This is, of course, extremely unlikely. You can name people or organizations to inherit your estate.

B. I leave the antique rocking chair I inherited from my aunt to Esther Whitman. If she does not survive me, I leave this gift instead to Stephanie Ann Doe.

2.2 Residual Estate.

A. I leave my residual estate (all the property that is subject to this will that does not pass by a specific gift) to my spouse, John Richard Doe.

B. If he does not survive me, I leave my residual estate to Stephanie Ann Doe and Charles John Doe.

(i) If at my death any of my surviving children named above is under the age of 27 years, my residual estate shall be held in a Family Pot Trust, to be administered under the terms of that trust, as set forth in this will.

(ii) If at my death all of my surviving children named above are at least 27 years old, my residual estate shall be divided into equal shares for each of my children and distributed to them directly.

C. If neither my spouse nor any of my children named above survive me, I leave my residual estate to Jennifer Rose Smith.

Only persons or organizations that are alive or in existence 45 days after your death can inherit under your will. Otherwise, their gift will go to the alternate beneficiary you've named. There are two reasons to include this language. The first is to clarify what would happen to your estate if you and your spouse died at the same time or it was impossible to tell who had died first. (Your estate would then go to your children.) The second is to make sure that people who die within a short time of your death don't inherit your property and leave it to other people in *their* wills, which might mean that your property would then go to people that you'd rather didn't get it.	2.3. **Beneficiary Provisions**. Any beneficiary must survive me for 45 days to receive property under this will. As used in this will, "survive me" means to be alive (if a person) or in existence (if an organization) on the 45th day after my death.
This means that if you leave a car or a house to someone, it comes with the loan or the mortgage.	2.4. **Encumbrances**. All personal and real property that I leave through this will shall pass to a beneficiary subject to any encumbrances or liens on that property.
If a minor child (such as a godchild or a friend) inherits from you, this lets the executor give the gift to that child's parent as a custodian. This avoids a probate guardianship if the gift is large. Fill in the age at which the custodianship should end, being sure to follow your state's law. (See "Custodial Accounts" in Chapter 3.)	2.5. **Gifts to Minors**. If the executor is directed to make a specific gift to a minor child, the executor may, in the executor's discretion, make the gift instead to the minor's parent, as a custodian for the minor under the applicable Uniform Transfers to Minors Act to hold for the beneficiary until age <u>21</u>, or to another adult of the executor's choosing to serve as custodian.

ARTICLE THREE: EXECUTOR

List the person (probably your spouse) that you've chosen to serve as your executor, plus one or two alternates.

After that comes a statement about bond. Unless you include it in your will, your executor might have to post a bond (like an insurance policy) with the probate court to ensure that he or she faithfully carry out his or her duties. It's an unnecessary expense for the estate and a hassle for the executor.

3.1. Nomination of Executor. I nominate <u>Charles Richard Doe</u> to serve as my executor. If he is unable or unwilling to serve as executor, I nominate the persons listed below to serve as my alternate executors, in the order listed:

First, <u>Jennifer Rose Smith</u>.

Second, <u>Joseph Arthur Doe</u>.

No executor shall be required to post bond.

State law grants executors certain powers to administer your estate. You are stating here that you want your executor to work with as little court supervision as possible, so that your estate can be settled as quickly and inexpensively as possible.

This is a list of powers that you're giving your executor, in addition to those granted by state law. You want your executor to have as much power as possible to take care of your estate so that he or she won't have to ask a probate judge for permission to do things that need to be done.

3.2. Powers of the Executor. My executor may take all legally permissible actions to have the probate of my will done as simply and as free of court supervision as possible under the laws of Missouri, including the filing of a petition in the appropriate court for the independent administration of my estate.

In addition to all powers and authority granted to my executor by operation of law, I grant my executor the following powers:

1) To retain property without liability for loss or depreciation.

2) To dispose of property by public or private sale, or exchange, or otherwise, and receive and administer the proceeds as a part of my estate.

3) To vote stock; to exercise any option or privilege to convert bonds, notes, stocks; or other securities belonging to my estate

into other bonds, notes, stocks; or other securities; and to exercise all other rights and privileges of a person owning similar property.

4) To lease any real property in my estate.

5) To abandon, adjust, arbitrate, compromise, sue on or defend, and otherwise deal with and settle claims in favor of or against my estate.

6) To continue or participate in any business which is a part of my estate, and to incorporate, dissolve, or otherwise change the form of organization of the business.

7) To employ professional advisers with respect to investing the assets of my estate and to treat any fees paid to such advisers as expenses of the administration of my estate.

8) To take any other action that may be necessary or appropriate for the proper and advantageous management, investment, and distribution of my estate.

ARTICLE FOUR: GUARDIANSHIP

This section documents your choices for the personal guardian of your children. You nominate the same guardians for all of your children.

4.1. **Nomination of Guardians**. If at my death a guardian is needed to care for my children, I nominate _Jennifer Rose Smith_ as the guardian of the persons of my children. If she is unable or unwilling to serve as guardian, I nominate the persons listed below to serve as guardian, in the order listed:

First, _Joseph Arthur Doe_.

Second, _Marilyn L. Johnson_.

This clause ensures that your guardian won't have to post a bond with the court, which is otherwise required to make sure that he or she carries out his or her legal duties.

4.2. **Waiver of Bond.** No bond shall be required of any guardian appointed in this will.

ARTICLE FIVE: FAMILY POT TRUST

If your children inherit from you while any of them is under the age you specified above, the assets you leave to your children are placed into a trust for their use. Until the youngest child turns a specified age, and the trust ends, the trustee will use these funds to provide for your children's daily needs. If a child dies before the trust terminates, his or her share stays in the pot trust and goes to the surviving siblings.

Your trustee is responsible for investing and distributing the trust funds.

Trust funds may be used for anything your children need while they are growing up. The trustee can spend more on one child than the others if necessary, but the trustee does have an obligation to treat all beneficiaries fairly. The trustee does not have to spend all of the income earned by the trust in any given year. Any income earned by the trust that is not distributed to the beneficiaries will be added to the trust principal.

The trust ends when your youngest child turns whatever age you've specified above. At that point, the trustee will divide the trust assets into one share for each

5.1. **Family Pot Trust**. Those assets distributed to the Family Pot Trust shall be held, administered, and distributed as follows:

A. **Beneficiaries**. The beneficiaries of the Family Pot Trust are <u>Stephanie Ann Doe and Charles John Doe.</u> If a beneficiary survives me but dies before the Family Pot Trust terminates, that beneficiary's interest in the trust shall pass to the surviving beneficiaries of the Family Pot Trust.

B. **The Trustee**. The trustee of the Family Pot Trust shall be <u>Jennifer Rose Smith.</u> If she is unable or unwilling to serve as trustee, <u>Joseph Arthur Doe</u> shall serve instead.

C. **Administration of the Family Pot Trust.** The trustee may distribute trust assets as he or she deems necessary for a beneficiary's health, support, maintenance, and education. Education includes, but is not limited to, college, graduate, post-graduate, and vocational studies and reasonably related living expenses. In making these payments, the trustee may pay or apply more for some children than for others and may make payments to or f surviving child. If there are no surviving children, the trust assets will go to your legal heirs—those who inherit your estate under the state rules of inheritance.

or one or more children to the exclusionof others. In determining the amount of these distributions, the trustee shall give consideration to all other income and resources that are known to the trustee and that are readily available to the beneficiaries for use for their education, support, and maintenance. Any trust income that is not distributed by the trustee shall be accumulated and added to the principal.

D. **Termination of the Family Pot Trust.** When the youngest surviving beneficiary of the Family Pot Trust reaches 27, the trustee shall distribute the remaining trust assets to the surviving beneficiaries in equal shares.

If none of the trust beneficiaries survives to the age of 27, then at the death of the last surviving beneficiary the trustee shall distribute the remaining trust assets to my heirs.

ARTICLE SIX: PROPERTY GUARDIAN

If your children own any property outside of the Family Pot Trust, the property guardian will manage it for them until they are 18.

If at my death, a guardian is needed to care for any property belonging to my minor children, I name Jennifer Rose Smith as property guardian. If she is unwilling or unable to serve as property guardian, I name Joseph Arthur Doe to serve instead. No property guardian shall be required to post bond.

ARTICLE SEVEN: GENERAL PROVISIONS

All trusts established in this will shall be managed subject to the following provisions:

	7.1. **Bond.** No bond shall be required of any trustee.
You are stating here that you want your trustee to be able to work as independently of any court supervision as possible.	7.2. **Court Supervision.** It is my intent that any trust established in this will be administered independently of court supervision to the maximum extent possible under the laws of the state having jurisdiction over the trust.
While your children's inheritance is held in trust, this language prevents the children from being able to pledge it to cover a debt and prevents creditors from seizing it to pay off their debts. This is called, aptly enough, a "spendthrift clause."	7.3. **Transferability of Interests.** The interests of any beneficiary of all trusts established by this will shall not be transferable by voluntary or involuntary assignment or by operation of law and shall be free from the claims of creditors and from attachment, execution, bankruptcy, or other legal process to the fullest extent permitted by law.
You want to make sure that the trustee has enough powers to properly manage the trust assets. This section lays out those powers. This provision allows the trustee to pay him or herself reasonable compensation out of trust assets for serving as trustee.	7.4. **Powers of the Trustee.** In addition to other powers granted a trustee in this will, a trustee shall have the power to: 1) Invest and reinvest trust funds in every kind of property and every kind of investment, provided that the trustee acts with the care, skill, prudence, and diligence under the prevailing circumstances that a prudent person acting in a similar capacity and familiar with such matters would use. 2) Receive additional property from any source and acquire or hold properties jointly or in undivided interests or in partnership or joint venture with other people or entities. 3) Enter, continue, or participate in the operation of any business, and incorporate,

liquidate, reorganize, or otherwise change the form or terminate the operation of the business and contribute capital or lend money to the business.

4) Exercise all the rights, powers, and privileges of an owner of any securities held in the trust.

5) Borrow funds, guarantee, or indemnify in the name of the trust and secure any obligation, mortgage, pledge, or other security interest, and renew, extend, or modify any such obligations.

6) Lease trust property for terms within or beyond the term of the trust.

7) Prosecute, defend, contest, or otherwise litigate legal actions or other proceedings for the protection or benefit of the trust; pay, compromise, release, adjust, or submit to arbitration any debt, claim, or controversy; and insure the trust against any risk and the trustee against liability with respect to other people.

8) Pay himself or herself reasonable compensation out of trust assets for ordinary and extraordinary services, and for all services in connection with the complete or partial termination of this trust.

9) Employ and discharge professionals to aid or assist in managing the trust and compensate them from the trust assets.

10) Make distributions to the beneficiaries directly or to other people or organizations on behalf of the beneficiaries.

This means that if any part of the trust is declared invalid, it won't affect the rest of the trust.

7.5. Severability. The invalidity of any trust provision of this will shall not affect the validity of the remaining trust provisions.

You sign the will and state that no one is making you do it.

Signature.

I, <u>Mary Ruth Doe</u>, the testator, sign my name to this instrument, this _____ day of _____ , ____ at _____.

I declare that I sign and execute this instrument as my last will, that I sign it willingly, and that I execute it as my free and voluntary act. I declare that I am of the age of majority or otherwise legally empowered to make a will, and under no constraint or undue influence.

Signed: _____
<u>Mary Ruth Doe</u>

Two people must watch you sign your will. You shouldn't use someone who might benefit from your will in any way. So don't use beneficiaries as witnesses. You and both witnesses should be together in the same room when you sign the will.

The witnesses need not read your will, but you must tell them that you intend this document to be your will.

Make sure each page is numbered and dated; then write your initials on each page on one of the blank lines where indicated. On the last page of your will, write in the date, and on the blank line after "at," fill in the city or county and state in which you are signing your will. Repeat this information in the blanks that appear

WITNESSES

We, the witnesses, sign our names to this instrument and declare that the testator willingly signed and executed this instrument as the testator's last will.

In the presence of the testator, and in the presence of each other, we sign this will as witnesses to the testator's signing.

To the best of our knowledge, the testator is of the age of majority or otherwise legally empowered to make a will, is mentally competent, and is under no constraint or undue influence.

just before the witnesses' signatures. Then sign it in the presence of the witnesses. Use exactly the form of your name printed on the will. The witnesses should state that they realize you intend this to be your will. They should then, in your presence, initial each page near the line you did, sign the last page in the space indicated for witnesses, and fill in their addresses.

We declare under penalty of perjury that the foregoing is true and correct, this _____ day of _____ , _____ , at _____ .

Name _____

Address _____

_____

Name _____

Address _____

_____

Name _____

Address _____

_____

■

Consider a Living Trust

. . . .

What you'll do here:

☐ Decide whether your estate plan should include a living trust.

☐ If yes, name trustees and beneficiaries for the trust.

☐ Learn which assets need to go into a trust and which don't.

. . . .

The will you just created is a terrific document and covers all the family estate planning basics. You've named guardians for your children and for their inheritance, left money or property to others, and stated your final wishes in other matters. You can now hire a babysitter and take that first trip away from the kids knowing that you've been a diligent and responsible parent.

When you get back from that trip (or maybe just from the movies), though, and are feeling relaxed and refreshed, here's another question: Would it make sense for your estate plan to include more than the basics?

A will is not always the least expensive or quickest way to transfer property to your children. That's because unless you do some estate planning in addition to writing a will, your estate will probably be subject to a probate court proceeding after your death. To spare your family the expense and delay of a probate proceeding, you can leave your property through a "living trust" instead of a will.

Avoiding probate is a good thing for families to at least consider. The real question is whether it is worth it to you to do the planning required to avoid probate now, or wait until later. If you just want to get the basics done at this point and postpone anything more until your children are older or until you acquire more assets, you may, with perfect serenity, skip this chapter. But if you'd like to learn more, read on.

Probate: A Judge Makes Sure the Right Things Happen

Probate is a court proceeding that takes place after someone's death. During probate, a judge checks to make sure that a will is valid and requires the executor to submit an inventory of the property subject to the will. Once that's been done and the executor has notified the proper people (including creditors) and paid debts and taxes, the executor can transfer what's left to the beneficiaries named in the will.

This process takes several months at a minimum—probate in many states can easily last up to a year—and can cost your estate thousands of dollars. And if you own property in more than one state, your estate will have to conduct probate proceedings in each of those states.

It's hard to say exactly how much the process will cost, because the cost of probate varies so much from state to state. If you live in a state that has adopted a set of laws called the Uniform Probate Code, probate will likely be quicker and cost less than in other states.

If you live in a state that's not listed below, the probate process will probably cost something close to 5% of the value of the estate going through probate.

Where Probate Is Less Painful			
(States that have adopted the Uniform Probate Code in whole or in part)			
Alaska	Hawaii	Minnesota	North Dakota
Arizona	Idaho	Montana	South Carolina
Colorado	Maine	Nebraska	South Dakota
Florida	Michigan	New Mexico	Utah

Lawyers' Fees

My clients often think of the cost of probate as a tax on their estate. It feels like one, especially in states that allow lawyers to charge a percentage of the estate's value in fees. But it isn't a tax. It doesn't go to a government. Most of it goes to lawyers who represent the estate in the probate process. (The rest consists of court filing fees, copying costs, and fees for various experts, such as appraisers.)

Your executor hires the lawyer. And the executor should understand, up front, how that lawyer charges for his or her services and how much the probate proceeding is likely to cost the estate. In some states, lawyers are allowed to charge whatever a court agrees is "reasonable."

In a few states, the lawyer's fees are a percentage of the value of the estate, often with extra costs tacked on—regardless of how much time and work a particular case takes. What really makes the fees mount up in these states is that it's the value of the gross estate that's counted. For example, if your house could be sold for $500,000, but you owe $450,000 on the mortgage, the probate court will count the $500,000 figure as the home's value, not the $50K that's actually owned by you and not the bank. In California, probating an estate worth $200,000 currently costs $7,000 in lawyers' fees; an estate worth $1 million costs $23,000; and an estate worth $10 million costs $113,000 to probate. And the lawyer and the executor can each collect a fee of that size from the estate.

For a simple estate, your executor might be able to negotiate a lesser fee. I know lawyers who charge for probate work on an hourly basis and agree that they won't go beyond the allowed fee. (They can't do that, anyway, because the percentage fees are the most that lawyers can charge, unless they can request payment for what are called extraordinary services.) Other lawyers will represent an estate for half of the state-set percentages or for a fixed percentage of the estate's gross value. Most lawyers, though, love the percentage-fee system because they get the full fee regardless of how much time the case requires. Probate is a high-profit service for them.

TIP

Probate has nothing to do with estate taxes. When you die, everything you own, whether it goes through probate or not, is tallied up for estate tax purposes. But until 2011, or until Congress changes the current law, only the very wealthy are subject to the estate tax. Currently, you can leave up to $2 million of property tax-free, plus an unlimited amount to your spouse without tax.

Will Your Assets Have to Go Through Probate?

Probate, fortunately, isn't required for everything you own. Any asset for which you've designated a beneficiary outside of your will won't be subject to probate. Some common examples include:

- IRAs and 401(k) plans
- life insurance policies
- annuities, and
- payable-on-death bank or brokerage accounts.

Also, any property you own with someone else and for which you have a right of survivorship won't be subject to probate. The right of survivorship, remember, means that when one co-owner dies, the survivor owns the property automatically, without probate. So if you own property with your spouse (or someone else) as joint tenants, it won't go through probate when the first owner dies. And depending on your state's property ownership laws, you may also own property with someone else as "tenants by the entirety" or as "community property with right of survivorship." Both of those forms of ownership also carry the right of survivorship. (In Chapter 2, "Forms of Ownership" discusses these forms of ownership and how to tell if you hold property in one of these ways.)

When you take away any assets that will pass without probate because you've designated a beneficiary or they will pass to a co-owner automatically, whatever's left is what must go through probate. In other words, generally only property that you own alone will go through probate. For most people, that means assets such as cash in the bank, investments, household property, and sometimes real estate.

> **EXAMPLE:** Mary, who lives in a community property state, owns a house and two checking accounts with her husband Arthur as a joint tenant. She also inherited a cabin the mountains from her mother, which she owns as her separate property. Mary wrote a will, leaving the cabin to her niece Stella. At her death, the cabin must go through probate so it can be transferred to Stella. The home and bank accounts, however, pass to Arthur automatically because he's the surviving joint tenant.

If the property that you have that would be subject to probate doesn't amount to much, you may even be able to avoid probate entirely under your state's "small estate" process. If the value of your probate assets is below your state's limit, those assets can transferred outside of probate by using either a simple affidavit procedure or a simplified probate procedure. The limit set by each state varies a lot. In California, for example, it is $100,000, but in Maine it's just $10,000. Pretty much anywhere, if you own a house by yourself, you'll be above the limit.

Should You Plan to Avoid Probate?

Most sane people do not want to enrich lawyers. But the main reason to avoid probate is that most families, especially young families, gain nothing by it. Probate takes thousands of dollars out of the estate—money that otherwise would go to the kids. Most families don't need a court to supervise the distribution of assets, because no one is fighting about the estate and there are no messy creditor problems to resolve. Waiting months or a year to distribute the assets to children is just a waste of time. Probate is also a public process, because wills must be filed in the probate court and become public, open to all who care to inspect them.

What Is a Living Trust?

A trust is a legal agreement, but I find that it makes more sense to think of it like a play. There are three different actors. One owns the property that will be placed in the trust and is called the settlor or grantor. One is going to manage that property while it is in the trust and is called the trustee. And one, called the beneficiary, gets to use the property that's in the trust or will eventually own it after the trust terminates.

The trust document is like the script. It states who will play each role (and names their understudies). It tells the actors what to do so that the play can be performed. It states what property will be held in the trust, who can use it, how it will be invested and spent during that time, and when the trust will end. And for the grand finale, it says who will get the trust property when the trust ends.

The Trust's Cast of Characters	
Settlor or Grantor	The person who contributes property to the trust.
Trustee	The person who manages the trust assets.
Beneficiaries	The person who benefits from the trust assets and also the person who receives property when the trust ends. They can be different people.

EXAMPLE 1: Irving and Rebecca (the settlors or grantors) set up a trust for the benefit of their three children (the beneficiaries). They appoint William, Rebecca's brother, to serve as the trustee. The trust document (the script) requires William to distribute $10,000 to each child on that child's 18th birthday and to give each child an equal one-third when the youngest child turns 21.

EXAMPLE 2: Marjorie (the settlor or grantor) establishes a trust for her nieces and nephews (the beneficiaries). Her brother Christopher is to serve as trustee. The trust funds may be used only for education and medical expenses not covered by health insurance. When the youngest beneficiary finishes college or turns 23, whichever happens first, the trust (the script) says that Christopher must distribute any trust funds that are left to the nonprofit organization Doctors Without Borders.

Trusts can be used to manage all sorts of property for all sorts of reasons. You may have heard of or met wealthy "trust fund babies," who are the beneficiaries of trusts that their parents created for one. You may have heard of land trusts, which hold property for the benefit of certain families or the public. You may have heard of the Social Security Trust Fund, where your social security payments are held, to be paid out to those currently eligible for benefits. (That's the idea, anyway.)

A living trust is just another kind of trust agreement. It is used only for estate planning. Both single people and families can use one. A living trust is sometimes called a will substitute because it is used, instead of a will, to determine who gets what and how the property is managed. (You'll still need a will, but I'll get to that later.)

In our living trust drama, one actor starts out playing all three roles. If you create a trust for your property (that means you are the settlor or grantor), you are usually also the trustee, the person who manages that property during your lifetime. You are *also* the beneficiary of the trust during your lifetime—the assets are to be used for whatever you need. The trust will state who gets the property after your death—probably your children (they become the beneficiaries then). It's called a "living trust" because you establish it during your lifetime, not after your death. The children's trust you created in your will (see Chapter 4), which is created only after your death, is called a testamentary trust.

You don't give up any rights to the property that you transfer to a living trust. Of course, it depends on how a particular trust is written (that's the script), but a well-drafted living trust allows you to do everything with your property after it's been placed in trust that you could do before—including buy, sell, borrow against, or give away assets. You can also change any of the trust's terms or revoke it entirely if you want to. You start out as both settler and trustee of the trust, but if you ever need help, others can step in and manage the trust assets for you—you don't have to play both roles forever.

People create living trusts because by putting property in the trust, it is not subject to probate when the settlor dies. Instead, the trustee takes care of the transfer of trust assets without probate court supervision. This means the assets can often be transferred much more quickly. A simple trust can be settled within a few months of the settlor's death. Probate, in contrast, takes six months to a year in most states, and much of that time is spent waiting for the probate court to do something.

There are usually some fees and expenses associated with settling a trust, but they are almost always less than those of a probate proceeding. Most trustees hire an attorney to help them figure out what to do and are charged on an hourly basis for this advice. But most of what needs to be done should be simple, such as dividing up the assets in the trust and distributing them equally to the trust beneficiaries or establishing a trust for children.

> **EXAMPLE:** Jackson and his wife Claudia decide to create a living trust as part of their estate plan. They are the settlors of the trust and contribute their property to it. During their lifetimes they will serve as trustees and manage the trust assets for their own benefit. After one spouse dies, the surviving spouse will serve as trustee alone. At the death of the second spouse, their four children will inherit the trust property in equal shares. There will be no probate necessary for the transfer of property in the trust.

RESOURCES

For a great overview of living trusts and how you might use them in your estate plan, see *Plan Your Estate*, by Denis Clifford and Cora Jordan (Nolo).

Do You Need a Living Trust?

When I give talks at community groups and preschools, I always ask people whether they've heard about living trusts. Usually, about 75% of the people in the room raise their hands. This is usually three times the number of people who have actually DONE an estate plan of any sort, mind you! There's a lot of trust talk in financial magazines, on television talk shows, and in the newspaper. Practically every week I get a mailing from some outfit or another offering a living trust seminar somewhere nearby. There's an industry out there that's tried to drum up anxiety about not having a living trust. It's worked.

Living trusts are often touted as an essential part of everyone's estate plan, but I respectfully disagree. There's no doubt that a living trust is an excellent probate-avoidance technique. But it's not the only one. Property with a right of survivorship accomplishes the same thing, and in Chapter 8 you'll learn how to transfer securities and bank accounts without probate, too. Most important, young (or middle-aged, for that matter) couples aren't likely to face probate any time soon.

There are times when avoiding probate isn't an issue. If you own your assets in a way that already avoids probate, a trust is unnecessary. For example, if you own your house as a joint tenant with your spouse or partner, then when one of you dies, the house will pass to the survivor automatically. Second, if you live in a state where probate has been streamlined, you don't need to use a living trust to transfer assets efficiently to your children; probate can do it just as well. Third, for some families, the probate process makes sense. If you have complicated credit problems or a difficult family, probate provides an effective way to resolve disputes, because a judge's decision about who gets what is final.

The truth is that if you're part of a family with young children and own a house, an insurance policy, a retirement plan, and a small savings account, your most pressing estate planning can be accomplished with a will. I don't think it can be said too often: A will does what you need to do most, which is nominate guardians and manage your children's money. Everything else can wait until later.

Here's how I encourage my clients to think about it: There are lots of times in a family when you need to make a choice between doing a good thing and doing the best thing. My house, for example, has leaky wooden-framed windows that probably came with the house when it was built in 1953. Every single year my husband reminds me that we would save money on our gas and electrical bills and have a better-insulated and much quieter house if we replaced them. And every year, it seems, we don't have a few spare thousand dollars floating around, so we postpone it. Do our windows need replacing? Yes! Do we need to do it right now? Apparently not, since we've been thinking about it for the last seven years. Fixing our windows would be the best thing—but replacing the hot water heater when it leaks, replacing the bathroom floor when it floods, and not killing the lawn are what we can manage at the moment.

So why is it that virtually all my clients create living trusts, even after I've given them my little speech about the leaky windows? It could be because I'm not very convincing. But I think the better answer is that they all live in California, where probate hasn't been reformed, and in the Bay Area, where even a modest house costs way too much. My clients calculate that a living trust can save their kids more than $20,000 in probate fees, someday. For them, it's worth spending an extra $1,000 now to save that money later.

But that doesn't mean that's the right answer for you. If you are lucky, housing prices aren't so astronomical where you live, and probate is not so expensive. If so, you can skip the rest of this chapter and go directly to Chapter 6.

Watch Out for Trust Scams

Sooner or later, you'll find a flyer on your doorstep or car, or at your church, advertising a "Low-Cost Living Trust Seminar." Watch out. There's nothing wrong with seminars on estate planning, even free ones. (I do those myself.) But some are only a pretext for a hard sell.

To get you to attend, an unscrupulous company will offer a living trust for a fraction of what an attorney would charge.

Often called "trust mills," these companies usually offer a one-size-fits-all trust that's churned out with minimal, if any, supervision by an attorney. To get you to buy one, they often use wildly inaccurate stories about the horrors of probate. Then, once you're really scared, they oversell the advantages of living trusts, implying that once you die your heirs will have little or nothing left to do to settle the estate (also not true).

The quality of the trusts sold this way is generally quite low. Clients have shown me trusts that don't have complete sentences or that just don't make sense. I've also had clients come to me with trusts that don't have any assets in them, or the wrong ones. (An empty trust does nothing to avoid probate.)

Worse, some trust mills use seminars as a way to pry personal financial information out of you. They forward this information to insurance agents, who use it, with high-pressure sales tactics, to try to sell inappropriate annuities and other insurance products that they don't need. (An annuity is a kind of insurance contract. You invest a certain amount of money; the company guarantees a fixed payment for a certain period or a lump sum at a future date. There's nothing wrong with an annuity, but many have big penalties for early withdrawals, offer high commissions to sales agents, and are inappropriate for seniors, who are often the target of these tactics.)

If you're approached by a low-cost trust operation, ask your state's attorney general's office and your state's bar association for any information about the company. Both groups sue trust mill operators, trying to shut them down. Another place to inquire is a local senior center—trust mills often focus on vulnerable seniors, and community centers may have information on local scams.

Living Trusts vs. Wills		
	Living Trust	**Will**
Privacy	Your trust is not a public record, and your trustee transfers assets without court supervision.	Your will is filed in the probate court and is a public record, and a judge supervises the settling of your estate.
Cost to set up	A bit more work than making a will; if you work with an attorney, costs more than making a will.	Simpler to set up; easily done without an attorney.
Hassle to set up	You have to actually transfer certain property to the trust. This requires filing deeds and filling out forms. It isn't extremely difficult, but it is work.	No extra forms need to be filled out, and no property must be transferred.
What you can do with it	Leave property. Name someone to manage trust assets if someday you can't.	Leave property. Name a guardian for your children.
Process after a death	Most trusts can be settled quickly, getting assets to the beneficiaries sooner than if there were a will.	Probate is usually necessary; costs more and takes longer than wrapping up a trust.

Creating a Living Trust

Here's the big picture: To create a living trust, you need to identify the actors who will play the three required roles, and you need to draft a script that sets out what will unfold as the trust plays out. You then have to sign and notarize the trust properly to make it legal. Once you've signed the trust, you also have to transfer certain assets into it by filling out the right forms.

Of course, that's a little like saying that all you have to do to buy a house is sell the one you own now, find one you like better, make an offer, have the offer accepted, get a loan, and move in. The devil is in the details.

Your first decision is going to be whether to draft the trust yourself or seek a lawyer's help. If you like to do things yourself, you're in luck. A young family with a few straightforward assets can put together a living trust that will avoid probate and properly manage assets for their kids. It's not that hard. You'll need to work with well-drafted forms, gather the important information, and figure out answers to nuts-and-bolts questions.

Not everyone likes to do things themselves, though. I'm sure that most of us are capable to changing the oil in our cars, for example, or preparing our own tax returns, but do we? If I'm describing you, take heart. A lawyer will be happy to help you.

If you're sort of in the middle, there's a third way: find a lawyer who will consult with you and help you understand the forms and the questions they raise, but let you do most of the work yourself.

RESOURCES

Two great products that you can use to draft your own living trust are *Quicken WillMaker Plus* (Nolo) and *Make Your Own Living Trust,* by Denis Clifford (Nolo).

WillMaker is software that asks you questions and then, on the basis of your answers, generates a living trust for you to sign. It will also help you prepare wills, durable powers of attorney, and living wills, and a letter explaining why you made the choices that you did.

Make Your Own Living Trust is a book that comes with a CD-ROM of all the forms you'll need to create a living trust that's right for you. It has helpful information on how to transfer assets into the trusts and manage trust assets over time.

In my opinion, you should talk to a lawyer if you fit into one or more of these categories:

- You own assets (including life insurance, retirement assets, equity in your home, and cash in the bank) worth more than $2 million now, or they're likely to be worth that much in the near future.

- You are married to someone who's not a U.S. citizen.

- You have children or separate property from a prior marriage.

- You own your own business.

- You own complicated assets, such as private company stock or an interest in partnerships.

- You have a child with special needs who will likely need life-long financial support.

- You want your estate plan to take care of aged parents as well as your children.

If any of these apply to you, a well-trained lawyer ought to be worth the fee. A good lawyer's judgment and experience will add value to your estate plan. The lawyer will ask you to think about issues that you haven't thought about and will draft a trust agreement that addresses them.

Here's what you'll be paying for:

- **Professional focus.** You'll have to get yourself organized because you're paying (a lot) for someone to sit down with you and think things through.

- **Project management.** A good lawyer will help you complete the estate planning process by setting deadlines and seeing that you meet them.

- **Guidance.** A lot of times, people aren't sure of the best way to structure things in a trust. For example, clients often ask me what an appropriate gift to a guardian might be or when a children's trust should end. Someone who has done hundreds of trusts can give you guidance on what might work best for you family.

- **Funding.** Lawyers can help you with the transfer of assets into a trust (an extra step that isn't necessary when you just do a will). This is straightforward for most people, but figuring out which forms to get and how to fill them out makes some of us nuts.

How much does it cost to get a living trust drafted by an attorney? Costs vary widely across the country, of course. But I've found that as a general rule, a trust will take about 10 hours of a lawyer's time. So a lawyer who charges $150 an hour will prepare a trust for about $1,500. Someone who charges $250 an hour might charge you about $2,500 for a trust. Trusts that cost significantly less than this may be drafted by paralegals under only nominal supervision by attorneys. Trusts that cost a lot more are usually drafted by law firms that offer fancy tax expertise (and often, fabulous offices) that is useful for the very wealthy, but probably not for you.

> **TIP**
>
> **Shop around.** When you're looking for an estate planner, make sure to ask whether the fee for a living trust includes the cost of preparing a will and durable powers of attorney for finance and health care (see Chapter 9 for more about those documents). These documents should all be created at the same time, so that your estate plan is comprehensive. Also ask whether the transfer of your house to the trust is included in the fee. If the attorney wants to charge on an hourly basis, keep looking. Most planners work for a flat fee, which is fairer to you and more predictable.

Casting the Play: Selecting Trustees and Beneficiaries

Whether you draft a trust yourself or hire a lawyer to help, you'll need to select the cast. The first role is easy: You and your spouse or partner are going to be the settlors of the trust. That means you'll be contributing property to the trust.

If you live in a community property state, you'll probably create one trust for both you and your spouse. If you live anywhere else, you might create one trust for each of you to hold your separate property.

The second role (the trustee) is also easy. This, remember, is the person who will manage the assets once they're in the trust. During your lifetimes, you and your spouse will be the trustees. You also need to name a successor trustee, who will take over as trustee at your death and transfer trust property to the beneficiaries you named in the trust. If you become ill and can no longer manage the trust assets, the successor trustee will manage the trust property for you.

Here's the good news: You've *already* selected a successor trustee in Chapter 3. When you worked through the issue of managing money for your children, you selected someone you felt would do a good, long-term job of managing your children's inheritance. That's who you should name as your successor trustee.

If you choose to use a living trust, then your trust, not your will, becomes the document that determines who gets what and how your children's inheritance will be managed. You'll still need a will to name guardians for your children and to take care of any property that isn't part of your trust, but the trust does all the heavy lifting now.

All the decisions you've already made about how you want to manage your children's inheritance will be written into your trust. The money manager you've chosen will be the successor trustee of your living trust. Your trust will say that if you die with young children, the assets should be distributed to a children's trust that's just like the one you created in your will in Chapter 4. Your successor trustee will manage the trust for your children until it ends. If you live a long and healthy life (and I sincerely hope that you do) and die when your children have become adults, the successor trustee's job will be different. There won't be a children's trust to manage, just assets to distribute as the trust directs.

EXAMPLE: Renaldo and Joan decide that for them, a living trust makes sense. They use Quicken WillMaker to create a simple living trust and name Leslie, Joan's sister, as the successor trustee.

They had already chosen Leslie to be the trustee for their family pot trust when they thought through their will in Chapter 4. Now they name Leslie as the successor trustee in their trust.

It will be Leslie's job to distribute the trust property to their children's trust and manage it for the kids until they grow up. They also create a simple will to name guardians for their kids and to make sure that any property that they own that's not in the trust still gets to the children.

Filling the last role, that of beneficiary, is also a piece of cake. During your lifetimes, you, as the settlors, are also the beneficiaries of the trust. You have complete control over the assets and can use them for whatever you want. After one of you dies, the surviving spouse is the sole beneficiary. After you both die, your children are the beneficiaries.

EXAMPLE: During Renaldo and Joan's life, they have full control over their trust assets. The trust says that if both of them die, all the trust assets go to their two boys in equal shares. If a child is over 30 when his parents die, that child will get his share outright and can invest and spend it as he wishes. If a child is under 30, his share will be placed in trust for him until he turns 30. Leslie, Joan's sister, is the successor trustee of the trust. She will manage trust funds for the boys until they both turn 30. If they are both over 30 when their parents die, she will pay the debts and taxes owed by Renaldo and Joan and distribute what's left, in equal shares, to the boys.

Transferring Assets Into the Trust

After you've created a living trust, there's one more step: You've got to transfer certain assets into it. This is called funding the trust. This is different from what happens after you create a will. (Nothing actually happens after you create a will; you just store it somewhere really safe. When you die, the executor figures out what you owned, and the fun begins.) But a trust doesn't do you any good at all unless you transfer assets into it during your lifetime. If those assets are outside of the trust when you die, a probate proceeding will be necessary for them. Having an empty trust is a complete waste of time and money, but lots of people end up with one. It's the most common thing that people do wrong.

> **EXAMPLE:** Fifteen years ago, Bertha set up a living trust and named her sister, Meg, as the successor trustee. She wanted to avoid making her three children go through the hassle of a probate proceeding. Bertha owned a house, a Fidelity investment account, a savings and checking account, and an IRA. Bertha didn't much like her estate planning attorney, who made her feel stupid when she asked questions. She signed all the papers and promptly forgot about the whole thing.
>
> When Bertha died, Meg went to a different estate planner to find out what she was supposed to do. After reviewing the title on the house and the statements for Bertha's accounts, the lawyer told Meg that Bertha hadn't transferred the house, the Fidelity account, or the bank accounts to the trust. Before any property could be transferred, Meg had to take the whole estate through probate.

What to Hold in Trust

Transferring assets into a trust is a minor hassle, but it's not impossible. The first step is figuring out what goes into the trust. Not everything you own goes into a trust. Only your big-ticket items should be transferred to the trust, and not even all of those.

Most families own two kinds of assets: those that would be subject to probate if they weren't in a trust, and those that would never be subject to probate no matter what. Your trust should hold only assets that would otherwise go through probate. The other assets stay outside the trust.

Here's how to understand the difference. Probate is supposed to be all about avoiding fraud. Put another way, courts supervise who gets what so that evil nephew Fred can't steal the house that you meant to leave to your daughter Sylvia. (This all goes back to merry old England and bad doings when the Lord died.) Assets that are subject to probate are assets, like houses, stocks and bonds, and cash, that don't have a designated beneficiary attached to them. Without court supervision, the theory goes, evil nephew Fred might be able to steal those from the rightful heirs.

Other assets, those that have a designated beneficiary, such as your retirement accounts and your life insurance policies, will never be subject to probate. No court supervises the proper transfer of those assets. No court needs to. If evil nephew Fred asks New York Life, for example, for a $1 million life insurance policy payout, New York Life is not going to give it to him if he's not the named beneficiary. If Fred tries to get Fidelity to turn over your IRA, he's going to strike out there, too, unless you named him as your beneficiary on the plan.

Take a look at the table below. The kinds of assets listed in the left-hand column will go through probate unless you arrange otherwise. Put them into a living trust, though, and they will be transferred by the trust's terms and won't be subject to probate court supervision. The assets listed in the right-hand column aren't subject to probate anyway, so they don't need to go into the trust.

What Goes Through Probate?	
Assets Subject to Probate	**Assets Not Subject to Probate**
Cash in the bank, either savings or checking	Payable-on-death accounts—can be used for bank accounts, securities, and, in some states, cars and real estate
Brokerage accounts	
Mutual funds	Retirement assets
Securities	Annuities
Household items	Life insurance proceeds
Property held as community property, tenants in common, or separate property	Property held with a right of survivorship: joint tenancy, tenancy by the entirety, community property with right of survivorship

Getting the Forms

If you want to transfer financial accounts to your trust, you have to notify the financial institutions that hold your money that you want to own the accounts as a trustee. They'll send you the proper forms to fill out. Banks will usually make you fill out the forms at the bank. Generally, all of the forms require you to fill in the name of your trust, the date it was signed, the names of the trustees, and the Social Security number of one of the trustees (this is used this as a tax I.D. number). You won't have to file separate tax returns for your living trust, but all financial institutions want a tax I.D. number, anyway.

To transfer a house into a trust, you have to file a deed that transfers ownership to yourself(ves) as trustee(s). If you work with an estate planner they'll usually file the deed for you. Some planners also transfer accounts for you, though often for an extra fee. Don't pay it; you can do it yourself.

Everyday checking and savings accounts are usually not put into trust because they aren't large enough to require a probate proceeding to transfer them at an owner's death.

> **EXAMPLE:** Renaldo and Clara finished their living trust. Then they transferred their house into it by filing a deed with their county. Now the deed identifies the owners as "Renaldo Jones and Clara Green Jones, as trustees of the Jones Family Trust, dated November 28, 20xx." They also transferred their Charles Schwab brokerage account to the trust by filing out a Trust Account Application that they downloaded from the Schwab website. Now their statements are sent to "Renaldo and Clara Jones, TTE" (that stands for trustee).
>
> Finally, they transferred their large savings account at the credit union to themselves as trustees by filling out a form at the credit union. Those statements also come to "Renaldo and Clara Jones, TTE." They don't bother to transfer their everyday checking account, which rarely holds more than $5,000.

You can't transfer any assets into the trust until you've signed and notarized the trust agreement. That makes sense, since a bank or other financial institution wouldn't let you transfer an account to something that doesn't yet exist. When you're creating a trust, just gather the forms you'll need. That way, you can sign the trust and fill out the forms at the same time, while you're thinking about it. People make more of the hassle factor than necessary. If you have enough assets to require a trust, you're smart enough to fund and maintain one.

Do You Still Need a Will?

If you decide to create a living trust, do you still need a will? Yes. But it will be a slightly different from the one in Chapter 4. That will is designed to be your main estate planning document. It instructs the executor to do the big jobs: divide up your assets properly and manage them for your children until they mature.

If you create a trust, though, you'll create a will that is coordinated with it. The two legal documents have to be consistent—otherwise, your family will have a mess on its hands. You don't want the trust leaving property to one person and the will leaving the same property to someone else. If you have a will already, don't worry; it's easy to create a new one. Any will states right at the beginning that you are revoking your previous will. (But also rip up the old one. That way there won't be any confusion about which one's valid.)

When you use a living trust to transfer property to your children, suddenly the will has a lot less work to do. One way to think of the relationship between the two documents is to think of the trust as a cup, holding your biggest assets to avoid probate, and the will as a saucer. It simply catches any property that doesn't make it into the trust and instructs the executor to pour it into the trust upon your death. This kind of will is called a pour-over will.

A pour-over will has three main jobs.

It gets property into the trust. A pour-over will directs the executor to transfer all the property that you own that's outside the trust into the trust after you die. That way, just one document (the trust) says who gets what. As long as the property that's outside of the trust isn't large enough to require a probate proceeding, transferring these assets is an easy task. If you forgot to put a big asset into the trust, though, the executor might have to go through probate to transfer that asset to the trust. And that, of course, wipes out the benefits you were hoping to get by using a living trust in the first place.

> **EXAMPLE:** Bertha, the settlor who died with an empty trust, left her trustee and executor, Meg, with a bit of a mess on her hands. Meg has to hire an attorney to probate Bertha's house, Fidelity account, and checking and savings accounts. At the end of the probate, these assets are transferred to Bertha's trust, and then Meg can distribute them in equal shares to her nieces and nephews. This process might take a year and will cost Bertha's children thousands of dollars in fees. Most of the time and money could have been saved had Bertha properly funded her trust.

It names guardians. Your will also nominates guardians for your minor children. That's the job most parents are most worried about. You can't do this in a living trust; it takes a will.

It names an executor. Your pour-over will names an executor and at least one backup executor. If you have a trust and fund it properly, your executor is not going to have to take your estate through probate. But the executor must still file an income tax return, pay debts and expenses, and take care of the logistics that are necessary after any death. Most people name the same person as executor and trustee, but they don't have to be the same person.

If you hire a lawyer to draft a living trust, make sure that you also receive a pour-over will go with it. If you decide to do it yourself, make sure that you use the forms provided to create a backup will, to leave any property outside of the trust to those you designate.

A backup will does a lot of what a pour-over will does. It names guardians and executors and deals with any property that you have outside of a trust. Instead of pouring into the trust, though, it just leaves the property to those you name in the will directly. One set of rules govern the trust assets and the will says who gets everything else. That also works. As long as it doesn't conflict with your trust, it gets your property to the right people, and that's the most important thing.

■

Name the Right Beneficiaries for Your Retirement Plans

What you'll do now:

- ☐ Figure out what retirement plans you've got and who the beneficiaries are now.

- ☐ Make sure that your retirement plans have the right beneficiaries from now on.

- ☐ Learn why you should convert old 401(k)s to IRAs.

- ☐ Consider converting your IRAs and 401(k)s to Roth plans.

F or years, I hope, you've been saving a chunk of each paycheck in some kind of a retirement account. These accounts offer tax incentives to help you squirrel away some money for retirement. Congress, when it came up with these tax breaks, really wasn't thinking of retirement accounts as a way to pass money along to heirs. The idea was that you were supposed to save the money during your working life and then spend it all during your retirement years, leaving nothing behind. Personally, I think that's an excellent plan. But it doesn't always work out that way. In fact, retirement accounts are in important part of an estate plan for at least five reasons.

First, the odds are that your retirement assets are one of the three biggest assets you'll be leaving behind, after your house and your life insurance policies.

Second, they aren't covered by your will or living trust—the person who gets your retirement money is the person you've named as your beneficiary for that plan.

Third, unlike the other assets you'll be leaving to your family, most retirement plan money is going to be subject to income tax when the money is withdrawn.

Fourth, this is the last money you want your children spending for college and other living expenses, because early withdrawals mean that the assets aren't growing on a tax-deferred basis. So it is important to make sure that these assets are managed carefully for them.

Last, but not least, as long as you handle them properly, these assets will be distributed after your death without going through probate.

Many books have been written on retirement plans. Many of them are huge or difficult to read—often both. Just the rules for taking money out of retirement plans (let alone the best way to put money into them) are complicated, and they change often. But for now, here's all that matters: Someday, hopefully far in the future, your family may inherit your retirement assets. So all I discuss in this chapter is what you should do now to make sure that when that happens, the process is as easy as possible. The big idea is that you want them to keep the money in your retirement accounts growing tax-free as long as possible.

RESOURCES

More on retirement plans. For a terrific overview of retirement plans, good advice on retirement planning, and all the rules for taking the money out of these plans, see *IRAs, 401(k)s, & Other Retirement Plans: Taking Your Money Out,* by Twila Slesnick and John C. Suttle (Nolo). Unlike many books on this topic, this one is neither huge nor difficult to read.

Alphabet Soup: Plans Explained

Broadly speaking, there are three types of retirement plans that most young families use to save for retirement (and a new one that many young families will use in the future). All three offer significant tax incentives to encourage you to save money now so you'll have it to spend when you retire. You might have more than one of each on your list, especially if you've changed jobs a few times. Old retirement plans have a way of piling up if you're not careful. (More on that later.)

> **TIP**
>
> **Get 'em together.** You've probably heard this before, but a good way to keep track of all of your retirment accounts is to put each statement in a binder, one section per plan. That way, all of the relevant information is in one place. Also, if you get tired of filing so many different statements, that might nudge you to consolidate them into only one or two accounts.

Traditional IRAs

IRA stands for Individual Retirement Account. You can set these up yourself to save and invest your earnings over your lifetime. At tax time, you can deduct the amount you contribute, up to a certain amount each year, as long as you are not also covered by your employer's retirement plan and your total income doesn't exceed a certain amount.

When you withdraw your money, it is subject to income tax. But by then you'll be retired, and your income tax rate will probably be lower than it is now. You may begin withdrawing money from these plans when you are 59½ years old. If you withdraw the money early you will generally be subject to penalties for early withdrawal, and then you'll pay income tax on top of that. You must begin to take money out when you turn 70½ years old. There are several varieties of IRA plans, but they are all variations on this theme.

401(k) Plans

Your employer sets these up and offers several investment choices. You contribute pretax money, deducted from your paycheck. That way, your taxable income is reduced by the amount you contribute. Some employers even contribute matching funds. The money grows tax-free in the account.

As with IRAs, you may begin withdrawing money from these plans when you are 59½ years old, and you must begin to take money out when you turn 70½ years old. Early withdrawals are also generally subject to penalties. When you withdraw money, it is subject to income tax.

If you've worked for a school or a nonprofit, you'll have a 403(b) plan. These are very similar to 401(k) plans except that they are governed by a different section of the federal tax law.

Roth IRAs

These are like traditional IRAs upside down. You make contributions with money you've *already* paid tax on. There's no tax deduction available for the contributions you make. And there's no mandatory withdrawal age. So what's so great about Roth IRAs?

When you withdraw the money, you don't pay tax on it. You take the tax hit up front, but all the growth of the funds is tax-free. If you can afford to create one, and you qualify to do so, this can be a terrific way to pass money along to your children.

Currently (2007), Roth IRAs are available to married couples filing jointly with an adjusted gross income of less than $160,000 and individuals filing separate returns with an adjusted gross income of $110,000 or less. These income limitations are indexed to inflation.

Roth 401(k)s and Roth 403(b)s

The newest options in the retirement planning world are the Roth 401(k) and Roth 403(b) plans. If your employer offers one, you can sock away a chunk of your salary and let it grow tax-free. Like a Roth IRA, you'll put money into the plan that you've already paid tax on, but future distributions will be tax-free. There are no income restrictions on who can participate. Not all employers offer this option, however.

Figuring Out Whom You've Already Named as Beneficiaries

There are a million books and websites that can help you figure out whether you're invested in the right plan for your family and saving enough for your retirement. But that's not the focus of our discussion. For estate planning purposes, the important thing is to understand who will get the money if you die before withdrawing it all.

First things first: You need to know what kind of retirement plans you've got at the moment and who will inherit them. In Chapter 2, you created a family inventory, and one of the categories was retirement assets. But at that point, I didn't ask you to figure out who the beneficiaries were for those plans. Just finding all those statements was enough, for a start.

But now, if you don't remember whom you named on these plans, it's time to find out. Some companies let you view your beneficiary designations online; others require a phone call to either your HR department or the plan administrator (for example, Vanguard or Fidelity) directly. When you get the information, you can fill it in on the "Family Retirement Assets: Current Beneficiaries" worksheet in the Busy Family's Toolkit.

Each plan asks you to name at least one beneficiary who would inherit the assets in the plan if you were to die with a remaining balance. You named this person when you filled out the form to create an IRA or enrolled in your employer's 401(k) or 403(b) plan.

Your primary beneficiary is your first choice to inherit the money in the retirement plan. If that person dies before you do, your secondary beneficiaries, sometimes called the "contingent" or "alternate" beneficiaries, will inherit the money. If you're like most people, you'll want to name your spouse as your primary beneficiary and your children as the secondary beneficiaries.

Because your will or a trust won't control how your retirement assets are distributed, you should make sure that your beneficiary designations are correct and current. If you've been divorced or married since you opened up a plan, or had children since then, the chances are you've got outdated or incorrect beneficiaries listed.

If you need to change your beneficiary designations, don't worry—it's a piece of cake. I'll discuss it at the end of this chapter.

Obviously, you don't want to leave these assets to the flat-out wrong person. That would be a careless mistake. But even if you simply want to leave these assets to your family, as most people do, it's worth understanding the best way to do so. Retirement plans have tricky rules about how money must be withdrawn and when. Worse, the rules are different for different beneficiaries.

Family Retirement Assets: Current Beneficiaries		
Retirement Plan	**Owner**	**Beneficiaries**
Vanguard Roth IRA, Number 123-456	Mary	Primary: John Secondary: Stephanie and Charles
TIAA-CREF 401(k)	John	Primary: Mary Secondary: Stephanie and Charles

Retirement 101: The Basic Rules of Choosing Beneficiaries

Your main job right now is to name beneficiaries to inherit any money you might leave behind in your retirement plans. Simple, eh? Well, for most people, it is.

But always keep the big picture in mind. Hopefully, when your beneficiaries inherit this money, they will want to keep it in the retirement accounts, growing tax-free, for as long as possible. If they don't, you want to make sure that they're not going to be able to withdraw the money until they're old enough to realize that doing so is generally a dumb idea.

To allow your beneficiaries the luxury of tax deferral, you want to avoid doing anything now that will later trigger IRS rules that will force your beneficiaries to withdraw money quickly. As you'll see, there a few mistakes you just don't want to make.

Different rules apply to traditional retirement plans (IRAs, 401(k)s) and to Roth plans. With traditional retirement plans, you must start withdrawing money after you've reached a certain age. These rules are there to make sure that you eventually pay the taxes you've been deferring, because you're taxed when you pull the money out. Roth plans, on the other hand, let you save for retirement with money that's already been taxed, so they don't have the same rules about mandatory distributions for you or for your spouse. When your kids inherit them, though, they'll be subject to mandatory distributions rules. Here are the basics.

IRAs and 401(k)s

You are required to start taking money out of your IRA, 401(k), or 403(b) by April 1 of the year after you reach the age of 70½. That's called your "required beginning date." The IRS allows you to defer paying taxes on the funds in your plan until then, but at that point you must start withdrawing money and paying income tax on it.

How much you take out is based upon your life expectancy. To simplify things quite a bit, you must take out a fraction of your account that's based on how long the IRS tables say someone your age is likely to live.

If you die before you're required to start taking money out of your retirement plan, your beneficiaries (other than your spouse) are going to have to start withdrawing money beginning in the year after your death. How much they must withdraw is based on their own life expectancies.

> **EXAMPLE:** When Miguel is 40, he inherits an IRA worth $150,000 from his Aunt Ethel. Miguel must start withdrawing the money the next year. The IRS tables say his life expectancy is 42.7 years, so he must take out $150,000/42.7, or $3,512.88, that year. Each year he must withdraw the current balance divided by a smaller number (the beginning denominator, minus 1 each year) until the account is exhausted. The second year, for example, he'd

have to divide the current balance by 41.7 to get the required distribution.

If you die *after* you turn 70½, the rules are a bit different. A beneficiary who is not your surviving spouse must take the distributions that you would have taken in the year of your death. After that, these beneficiaries must take money out based on their own life expectancies, until the account is depleted.

Roth IRAs and Roth 401(k)s

Roth IRAs (and now, Roth 401(k) and 403(b) plans) are different from traditional IRAs. Remember, with these accounts, you pay the tax first, then invest the money. You don't get an income tax deduction when you contribute the money, as you do with traditional IRAs. The money, though, grows tax-free, and there are no required withdrawals. That means that if you don't spend this money, it can continue to grow tax-free for your entire life, and you can leave it to whomever you wish.

Even though you don't have to withdraw money from your Roth account, your beneficiaries may have to. It depends on who's doing the inheriting.

- **Your spouse** can roll the money into his or her own Roth IRA and keep saving the money tax-free. Surviving spouses are not subject to any required minimum distribution rules and will pay no tax on the money once it's been withdrawn.

- **Your children** will be subject to the same required distribution rules that apply to IRAs and 401(k)s. This means that provided the plan permits it, they will have to begin taking money out one year after your death, but these payments will be stretched out over their expected lifetimes. Again, the money can continue to grow tax-free until the funds are exhausted, and no tax is due when it's withdrawn. What's really great is that if your beneficiaries need to pull the money out to buy a mortgage or deal with a medical emergency, they can do so, with no tax penalty.

EXAMPLE: Jonathan contributes to a Roth IRA for the last ten years of his life, without ever withdrawing any money from it. He names his wife, Julie, as the primary beneficiary of the account. At Jonathan's death, Julie rolls the inherited Roth IRA into a Roth IRA in her own name. She lives another 20 years and never withdraws any money from the account. She names Tamar, her daughter, as the beneficiary.

When Tamar inherits the account, she must begin withdrawing funds. She is 35 when she inherits the money, so her life expectancy is 48.5 more years, according to the IRS tables. She must start taking out a small fraction of the account's total value each year for the rest of her life. No income tax is due on these withdrawals. And if she needs more of the money, it's hers, tax-free.

Naming Your Beneficiaries

I really can't imagine who writes IRS regulations, but I'm pretty sure they're not originally from this planet. Get this: You can designate any person or organization that you wish as a beneficiary, but only certain beneficiaries get to withdraw the money from your plan slowly, over time, which is generally what you want them to do.

These lucky beneficiaries, who can stretch out distributions based on their life expectancies, are called "designated beneficiaries," and only the IRS can tell you who they are. If your beneficiaries don't qualify as designated beneficiaries under IRS rules, too bad. They'll have to withdraw all of the money within five years.

First of all, know that your spouse and your children qualify as designated beneficiaries. So if they're the only ones you want to name, you don't have anything to worry about. Any "natural person," in fact, can be a designated beneficiary. That excludes organizations and businesses.

Name *Somebody*!

Your worst option is naming no one. If that happens, a quick payout will be required. If you die before you are 70½, and name no one as a beneficiary, the beneficiaries of your estate must withdraw all of the money within five years of your death. If you die after you are 70½, the beneficiaries of your estate will have to withdraw the money based on your age (which means a lot more quickly than they would have if you'd named them directly).

That means your retirement plan assets won't be able to keep growing tax-free. Quite the contrary, there will be steep income taxes to pay when the withdrawals are made. Worse, the money will go to your estate, which means a probate proceeding will be necessary to transfer the assets.

Some plans use your spouse as a default beneficiary if you don't name one. But don't rely on that option. If your plan doesn't have this default rule, the money would go to your estate.

Your Spouse

If you are married, name your spouse as the primary beneficiary. For most families, this makes sense both financially and emotionally. Spouses get special benefits that other beneficiaries of inherited retirement assets don't. Only spouses can defer withdrawal of the assets until they turn 70½ and name new beneficiaries to boot. Unless they need the money right away, this continued tax deferral is a terrific benefit. (Because all of these rules are a matter of federal law, they don't apply to registered domestic partners, whose rights are recognized only by certain states.)

Surviving spouses have two options that no one else gets. They can:

- Keep the plan in the name of the deceased spouse. This way, the survivor can take distributions over his or her own life expectancy, but beginning in the year that the deceased spouse would have turned 70½. If you are older than your deceased wife, for example, you can wait until she would have been 70½ to start withdrawing money. If the survivor wants to withdraw money right away, there's no penalty for early withdrawals. Some plans allow the survivor to name a beneficiary for an account kept in the deceased spouse's name; some don't.

- Roll the assets into the survivor's own IRA and defer any withdrawal until the survivor turns 70½. The survivor can also name new beneficiaries of the rollover account.

Your Spouse's Rights

As a general rule, if you want to name someone other than your spouse as the primary beneficiary of your retirement plan, you should get your spouse's consent in writing. Here's why.

IRAs. If you live in a community property state, your spouse may have some rights to the money in your IRA even if you don't name him or her as the beneficiary. A spouse who doesn't consent to a beneficiary designation could claim half of the account when the first spouse dies.

401(k)s. Under federal law, your spouse is entitled to inherit all of the money in your 401(k) or 403(b) plan unless your spouse signs a waiver consenting to your choice of someone else as a beneficiary.

 SEEK ADVICE

Get help when you inherit. Spouses who inherit retirement assets should seek professional advice before they take over the accounts. The rules governing retirement assets change often, and there are deadlines for making some decisions. Worse, a spouse who accidentally fails to take a required distribution within a certain period of time may be deemed to have decided to roll over an account, even if that was never intended.

Your Children

Who comes next, after your spouse? Most parents want to leave these assets to their children. Here's where it can get a little complicated.

If your children are under 18, they can't own these assets directly. If you just write down their names as beneficiaries, and then you die, a court will have to name a property guardian to manage that account for them until they're 18. After that, they'd be able to do financially unwise things, like take out all of the money in the account. It would then be taxed as ordinary income. Then, they might blow the money on something silly. Ouch.

Here's where having a coordinated estate plan really helps. Instead of naming your children directly, you can instead follow one of these strategies:

- Name a custodian for them, under your state's Uniform Transfers to Minors Act. That will provide management for the assets until age 21 in most states, 25 in a few. (See Chapter 3.)

- Better yet, if you've created (in your will or living trust) a trust to manage their money, name it as the secondary beneficiary. Under IRS rules, the age of the oldest beneficiary, usually your oldest child, will be used to figure out how much each beneficiary must take out of the plan each year, and then the distributions will be divided among the kids (if the trust has more than one child as beneficiary) according to the trust's rules.

WARNING

Check your plan's rules. Even though leaving your retirement plan to a trust for your children would allow them to stretch out withdrawals over the lifetime of the oldest child by IRS rules, some plans still might require the trust to withdraw all the money within five years. Plans can be more restrictive than what the IRS rules allow. Be sure that you know how your plan handles this.

Multiple Beneficiaries

It's generally not a good idea to leave a retirement plan to more than one person at a time directly—say, to three adult children. (It's okay to leave the plan to a trust that benefits more than one person.) If you do, your good intentions could create a headache for them. Here's what happens: If they don't split up the account by September 30th of the year following your death, then the age of the oldest beneficiary is the one that they all have to use to determine the required distributions. That means the money must be pulled out more quickly than it would be if each beneficiary could use his or her own life expectancy.

> **EXAMPLE:** Clara decides to leave her IRA, worth $300,000, in equal shares to her much older partner, Jason (aged 65), and her two daughters, Jane and Rita (aged 8 and 10). She names Jason as the custodian for Jane and Rita's shares. Clara dies the next year.
>
> The plan allows beneficiaries to use the life expectancy rule when distributing the money. Because Jason is the oldest beneficiary, the account must be distributed over his life expectancy. He will be 67 in the first distribution year, making his life expectancy (from the IRS tables) 19.4 more years. So to calculate the required distribution from the account, the beneficiaries divide the account balance ($300,000) by 19.4 years. That yields a result of $15,463.92, which is how much must be withdrawn in that first year.
>
> If instead, Jane, Rita, and Jason had each inherited separate accounts, Jane's required distribution would be $100,000/72.8 years = $1,373.63, and Rita's would be $100,000/70.8 years = $1,412.43.

It's possible for the beneficiaries to avoid this problem. If they get timely advice from someone who knows the rules, such as a financial adviser, accountant, or tax attorney, they can split the accounts up before September 30th of the date of death. If they do that, they can base required withdrawals on their own life expectancies.

You can also prevent problems by splitting up your accounts now and leaving each beneficiary a separate account. The downside to doing this is that it will cost you more in administrative fees, because each account will be administered separately.

> **TIP**
> **Don't name a charity along with someone else as beneficiaries of an IRA or 401(k).** Because the charity isn't a "designated beneficiary," the other person will be subject to the five-year withdrawal rule.

A Trust

Married couples often name a trust for their children as the secondary beneficiary of their retirement plans. (They name each other as primary beneficiaries.) Single parents often name a trust for their children as the primary beneficiary. That's generally a good plan, as discussed above. (See "Your Children," above.)

A trust for your spouse is a different thing altogether. Naming a trust for your spouse as the primary beneficiary of your retirement accounts, instead of your spouse directly, is not something to do casually. If done with the help of an estate planning attorney and coordinated with a carefully drafted estate plan, it can be a way to maximize a couple's ability to save or defer estate taxes at the death of the second spouse. But most people don't need to worry about estate tax—under current law, federal estate tax isn't a concern unless you plan to leave more than $4 million to your children.

Naming a trust as a beneficiary has some serious drawbacks:

- **No rollover.** Even if your spouse is the beneficiary of the trust, he or she will not be allowed to roll over plan assets into his or her own IRA and defer distributions until he or she turns 70½. (It's possible that a surviving spouse could take plan distributions and roll them over into an IRA, but that's why this is an area fraught with difficulties.)

- **No splitting.** If there are multiple trust beneficiaries, they won't be able to split the account into several individual accounts after your death. This means that they can't each use their own life expectancy to determine minimum distributions.

- **Complexity.** If someone other than your spouse is the beneficiary, that person will have to take out minimum distributions over their expected lifetime (or over five years, depending on the plan), and then the money will be subject to the trust's terms.

Charities, Businesses, and Other Organizations

Organizations such as a charity or a business are NOT designated beneficiaries under IRS rules. Again, that means that the money will have to be taken out within five years after it's inherited and won't be able to keep growing tax-free over the long term.

TIP

Sometimes, your survivors can fix your mistakes. The designated beneficiary of your plan doesn't have to be determined until September 30th of the year following your death. That means that sometimes, mistakes can be fixed before an accelerated payout is required. Now, forget I said that. It's much better not to make those mistakes in the first place.

A Little Housekeeping: Clean Up Your Retirement Plans

A great thing to do now to avoid headaches for your family later is to consolidate your retirement plans.

Roll Over Those Old 401(k) Plans

First, roll your old 401(k) plans into an IRA. Many people do this routinely when they leave one job and start another. But many don't.

I have clients who have three or four of these plans out there. If you roll them over during your lifetime, you'll gain control over where and how to invest your money. If you don't roll them over, your old company will continue to invest these funds in its 401(k) plan, which may be limited to a small group of funds and may be heavily invested in the company's own stock. Worse, you may discover that the company's moved the entire account somewhere else and neglected to tell you.

> **EXAMPLE:** Sarah had a 401(k) from her a former employer that was managed by a large brokerage company, Old Reliable Investing. Ten years after she left that job, her former employer moved the 401(k) account to a different company, New Advantages Investment. She learned about the transfer only when she got an account statement that showed her Old Reliable balance as zero.
>
> After repeated phone calls to her former employer, she was told that the account had been moved to New Advantages, but not what her account number was. Her former employer promised to contact New Advantages so that it would forward her the forms for a rollover, but never did so. Finally, Sarah hired an attorney to help her move her money.

Starting in 2008, you will be able to roll 401(k) money over into Roth IRAs, provided you qualify under the IRS's income limits. (See "Alphabet Soup: Plans Explained," above.)

If having control over your money isn't a big enough incentive to get your old accounts cleaned up, consider this: By rolling your old 401(k) accounts over now, you'll also make it easier for your spouse to roll them over into his or her own IRA if you die first. If the funds are still in an old 401(k), your family will have to work with plan administrators in a company that they may have had no dealings with for many years. The company may no longer even be in business—in which case it probably transferred management of its 401(k) plan to another company entirely. By transferring your old 401(k)s now into IRAs, your family won't have as much to do when you die. The company that manages the IRA now can continue to manage it for them when they inherit it and has an incentive to keep them happy to avoid losing the business.

Consolidate Your IRAs

Also consider consolidating your existing IRAs into one or two accounts. This will make it a lot easier to figure out how your investments are doing. You'll also save yourself duplicate fees and lessen the onslaught of mail you receive each month. And you'll make it easier on your surviving spouse or children to consolidate and manage their inherited accounts. It's surprisingly easy for survivors to entirely overlook an account if there are a lot to keep track of.

Filling Out the Forms

Plan administrators all have their own forms for you to use to designate your primary and secondary beneficiaries. You can also get a form to change your current beneficiaries. If you need that one, you can often download it from a company's website.

Every company's forms are a little bit different. But they're all trying to get you to name a primary beneficiary and a secondary (backup) beneficiary. Below is a cheat sheet that you can use to make sure you're naming the right people in the right way.

By the way, it's always a good idea to name your spouse by name (not just by writing "my wife," for example). You could, after all, have a different spouse someday, and you don't want any confusion over whom you meant to name.

If you're not sure whether to name a custodian or a trust to manage your children's inherited retirement assets, take a look at Chapter 3, where it's discussed in detail.

On many beneficiary forms, there's a box that you can check to add something called a "per stirpes" stipulation or "Right of Representation" to individuals you name as contingent beneficiaries. This means that if the named person doesn't survive you, but leaves behind children, those children would share the deceased parent's share, equally. I think it's a better idea to write down exactly what you want to do and not use their check-boxes.

Completing a Beneficiary Form	
Beneficiary	**How to Fill Out the Form**
Spouse	My spouse, Jane E. Jones, born on January 13, 19xx.
Children	**If as a custodial account:** To my children, Charles J. Jones and Evelyn M. Jones, in equal shares. Any benefits becoming distributable to a child under the age of 21 years [*this age varies by state*] shall be distributed to Rosalie L. Smith, as custodian under the Uniform Transfers to Minors Act of the state in which that custodian resides. *You can name a different custodian for each child if you wish. To look up the age at which a custodial account in your state must end, see Chapter 3, "When a Child Receives Property Held by a Custodian."* **If in trust:** To the trustee of the Jones Family Trust, created by my will dated April 4, 20xx. *OR* To the trustee of the Jones Family Trust, created on April 4, 20xx.

Get Enough Life Insurance

What you'll do here:

☐ Determine whether you need life insurance, what kind, and how much.

☐ Learn how to name the proper beneficiaries.

L ife insurance is an important part of nearly every family's estate planning. Some clients who come to my office have already bought insurance policies. Most times, though, it's only when we're discussing how to manage money for children that the idea of life insurance begins to make sense to people.

Often, when families fill out a financial questionnaire (you did one in Chapter 3, called "How Much Could Your Kids Inherit?"), they find that there wouldn't be much cash available for minor children. For many families, all of their assets are either tied up in their house (which could be hard to sell) or their retirement plans (bad idea to liquidate). What they need is a quick source of cash for their kids in case of unexpected tragedy. That's one of the things that life insurance is for. The right kind of life insurance is the cheapest, surest way to make sure that if you're not around, your kids will have enough money to grow up comfortably and get a college education.

Do You Need Life Insurance?

If you have children who rely on you for support, you need to make sure that there is enough ready cash to provide for their needs, both immediate and long term, in case you die unexpectedly. Life insurance is a terrific way to provide that cash, but not all families need it. If you have significant cash or equity savings (enough, at the very least, to pay off your mortgage), an extended family who would step in and take care of supporting your children, investment properties that could be sold quickly to raise money, or a pension plan that will provide adequate benefits to your family, then you might not need life insurance to fill the gap.

Here's what life insurance can offer young families:

Immediate cash after a death. This money can be used for last illness and funeral expenses and to pay any remaining debts and taxes of the deceased parent. If most of your assets are locked up in things that would be difficult to sell quickly (like a house, a business, or a collection of antiques) or in retirement assets that it would be a bad idea to liquidate, insurance money makes sense.

Tax-free money. The beneficiary doesn't have to pay income tax on life insurance proceeds except in certain, rare, circumstances.

Replacement of a lost income. If a working parent dies, insurance can allow a stay-at-home parent to continue staying home.

Money for childcare and domestic services. This can allow a breadwinning parent to continue working while hiring help to take care of the children and household.

Probate avoidance. As long as you don't name your estate as the beneficiary of your policies (and you shouldn't), insurance proceeds aren't subject to probate court proceedings.

Money for children with disabilities. Parents of children with special needs know that they need to provide money for the long-term care of their children. Insurance policies can provide this, as long as the proceeds are paid into a special needs trust for the benefit of the child, not to the child directly.

Estate tax reduction. If you're concerned about estate taxes, you can transfer your life insurance policies to a trust. The money will be paid to a surviving spouse or to children but won't be part of your taxable estate. Under current law, only about 1% of Americans die with taxable estates, so this isn't likely to be a concern for you.

EXAMPLE: Loren and Sarah are in their 30s and have two children, aged three and six. Like most families, most of their money is tied up in the house and their retirement plans. They have enough money in their savings account to cover three months of normal expenses. They decide to purchase life insurance polices for both of them.

Loren would want to be able to continue working, so Sarah's policy needs to pay out enough money so that Loren, at the very least, could hire enough childcare to take care of the kids during the day, Monday through Friday. Sarah would want to be able to stay home full time, so Loren's policy needs to pay out enough money to support the family for at least 15 years. They also want to make sure that if they were both to die at the same time, there would be enough money to get both kids through a public college.

What Is Life Insurance?

Life insurance is a contract between you and an insurance company. At its most simple, the deal works like this: In return for your annual payments, called premiums, they agree to pay out money, called a death benefit. For the insurance company, it's a bet—if you don't die before they have to pay out, they make money. If you die, and they have to pay out money, they don't. Of course, they issue policies to many people, so the risk of any one payout is spread out over a large pool of insured people. As long as *enough* people don't die while they are insured, the insurance company makes a tidy profit. (Earthquakes, hurricanes, and other catastrophes put great strain on insurance companies, for obvious reasons.)

The younger and healthier you are, of course, the better bet it is for the company. As you get older and your health declines, insuring your life gets riskier. The insurance companies know the odds. So it costs less to purchase insurance when you're young than it does when you're older. To put it another way, you get a huge discount for planning ahead. (See "The Older You Are, The More It Costs," below.) Many types of insurance policies have a level premium for the life of the policy, which means that you'll be able to lock in the lowest possible rate by buying the policy now.

People who put off buying life insurance pay more for it. A 45-year-old man will pay higher premiums for a life insurance policy worth $500,000 (about $700 a year) than he would have if he'd bought that same policy when he was 30 (about $300). It makes sense if you think like an insurance company. They have to charge him more to cover their risk of actually paying that $500,000. From their perspective, it's a lot more likely that he'll die in the next, say, 20 years than it would have been had he purchased that same policy 20 years before.

Life Insurance at Work

Many people get life insurance as a work benefit. Often the coverage is equal to one or two times their annual salary. Someone who earns $50,000 a year, for example, might get a policy that would pay $50,000 to $100,000 as part of the benefits package. At some companies you can even buy additional insurance for yourself or your spouse and have a small amount of your paycheck deducted to pay the premium.

There's nothing wrong with work-based life insurance—if it's offered by your company, take it. It isn't a good idea to depend on it entirely, though. If you get laid off or leave your job (and, let's face it, the odds of that happening are probably much higher than the odds of you dying), you'll lose that insurance. Then you'll find yourself shopping around for a policy when you're older than you are now. And that means the policy will cost you more.

Life Insurance Primer

Life insurance salespeople can offer you many different kinds of insurance policies. (Some, for example, are investments as well as insurance contracts.) I'm sure that each has its value. I've tried valiantly to sit through sales presentations with rapt attention, but I always lapse into a daze after about 15 minutes. I'm sure I have no future in the insurance industry (and now, no insurance salespeople will ever take me out to lunch), but I have only one thing in mind for my clients: life insurance that costs the least, pays out the most, and lasts only as long as they'll need it. From that point of view, one kind of policy offers the best value for the least investment: term life insurance.

Term life insurance is the simplest form of insurance. You agree to pay premiums for a certain period of time (the term). The company agrees to pay your family a certain amount of money (the death benefit) if you die during that term. If you don't die during the term, they pay nothing. If you do die during the term, your family gets the death benefit. For most term policies, the premium stays the same throughout the term, so you lock in the lowest rate if you buy it while you're young. If you stop paying the premiums, the policy lapses; you don't get your money back.

Because term life insurance is so simple and because the odds of young, healthy people dying are so low, it is cheap compared to policies that last your whole life and that also serve as an investment.

These policies are usually sold in 10-, 15-, 20-, and 30-year increments. Buy one that will last until your youngest child turns 21. After your youngest is in college, life insurance will serve a different purpose in your family—providing for your surviving spouse or equalizing your estate among adult children—or maybe none at all.

> **EXAMPLE:** Loren and Sarah decide to buy a term life insurance policy. Because their younger child is only three, they decide that a 20-year policy makes the most sense. When he turns 23, his sister will be 26. By then they hope that both of them will have made it through college. For Loren and Sarah, providing cash for young children is the primary reason to buy the policy, so they won't need life insurance once their kids are grown.

Okay, when might you want something other than term insurance? There are a couple of common situations. If you want a policy that lasts after your children are adults, consider buying

Types of Life Insurance		
Type	**General Features**	**Variations**
Term	The policy lasts for a specified period of time, usually 10 to 30 years, and pays out a fixed amount at the policyholder's death.	**Renewable**. You can extend the term without another medical exam. **Convertible**. You can convert your term policy to a permanent policy. That means that instead of the policy ending at a certain point, you can convert it to one that lasts your whole life.
Permanent	The policy lasts your entire life, as long as the premiums are paid up. Policies often include an investment component. Over time, a cash value for the policy builds up. Put another way, part of the premium you pay covers the risk of insuring you, and the rest is like an enforced savings account that the insurance company invests for you. You are usually able to take out loans against the cash value of the policy, and if you terminate the policy, you can cash it in for its "surrender value." As long as you don't take the money out, it grows tax-free. When you die, these policies generally pay out only the death benefit. Some also pay your family the cash value you've accumulated, but those policies cost more.	**Traditional whole life.** You pay a fixed premium for a fixed benefit. **Universal life.** The policy builds up a cash reserve, but you can vary the premiums and the benefits over time. **Variable life.** Your death benefit and the cash value of the policy vary depending upon how the company's investments perform. **Variable universal life.** These policies combine the ability to vary your premium payment and death benefit (like universal life) with the investment flexibility of variable life insurance. **Last survivor life ("second to die").** These policies insure two people but pay benefits only when the second one dies. They are generally used to pay estate taxes for wealthy families. **Single-premium whole life.** You buy the whole policy with one lump sum. This requires a large up front payment, but it's useful if you want to give a policy to someone else and not worry about the premiums staying paid up.

permanent life insurance or a term policy that you can convert to a permanent policy. If you like the idea of enforced savings, think about a permanent policy that allows you to pull money out later or borrow against the policy at a good interest rate to help you save money for the future. If you have a child with special needs, and need to make sure that your policy will always be available to support them, you should purchase permanent life insurance. (See "If You Have a Child With Special Needs," below.)

How Much Is Enough?

Once you've figured out what sort of policy would work best for you, you've got to decide how much of a death benefit you'd like to provide for your family. In my years of practice, I've heard many different theories about the best way to figure out the best amount for any given family. Every insurance salesperson and financial planner seems to have a favorite calculator or ratio.

I think it's worth exploring some of the different approaches to insurance calculations here, but the real answer for busy families is, "Buy as much as you need. If you can't afford that much, buy as much as you can afford. As soon as you can." And feel good about it. If a $1 million policy would take care of your family best, but you can only afford $500,000 worth of coverage, buy that. That's still $500,000 more for your family than they had without any insurance in place.

The Income-Multiplier Method

One simple way to calculate your insurance needs tries to replace lost income over a period of time. One figure I've heard frequently is six to ten times your annual salary. So if you earn $50,000 per year, you'd want $300,000 to $500,000 worth of life insurance. But this rule of thumb might not work for you. Maybe six to ten years isn't enough time for your family to be supported by insurance. Maybe your current income isn't sufficient, so you wouldn't want to use it as a benchmark. And this model doesn't value a stay-at-home parent's work at all.

Online Calculators

Another approach takes a look at your overall financial situation, including your expected short-term and long-term expenses, current salaries, current savings, and educational needs for your children. There are lots of calculators on the Web that will help you do this. One that I like is on the Motley Fool website (www.fool.com).

After you plug in basic financial data, the calculators compare your current funds with the total capital needed and calculate how much insurance you'd need to fill the gap between what you've got and what you'll need for as many years as you've specified. It's hard to tell what assumptions these calculators are making to come to their conclusions, or whether their estimates for investment returns and inflation are good ones. I used the same $50,000 salary figure in several of these online calculators for 20 years of income replacement—and was told I needed from $625,000 to $1.1 million of insurance.

A Look at Your Lifestyle

Another way is to take a look at what you're spending now, and then think about how this would change if you or your partner were to die. You might spend less on food but more on daycare, for example. The surviving spouse might need to pay off the mortgage in order to continue staying home with the children. Someone working part time might have to find a full-time job. This analysis focuses, as I think you should, on what kind of life and lifestyle you'd want for your family if one or both of you were to die. Once you get a rough idea of what it would cost your family to live for a month, you can start figuring out how much insurance to get.

Several financial planners I know use variations on this last approach. They want their clients to get a policy with proceeds that could generate enough income to pay off existing debts and cover the household's monthly expenses without dipping into the principal. A family with $50,000 in outstanding debts and $4,000 of monthly expenses, for example, needs $48,000 a year in income from investments to cover expenses, and more to pay off that debt. If they had $1 million invested at a 5% rate of return, that would generate $50,000 a year, less fees. If they got a policy worth $1.1 million, they'd be able to pay off the debts first and invest the rest. If they could get a better rate of return than 5%, they'd have more money to spend. If they could afford it, each parent should get a $1 million term life insurance policy.

> **EXAMPLE:** Loren and Sarah decide to get a term policy. For advice on how much they should purchase, they go see a financial planner. She advises them to get at least a $600,000 20-year term policy on Loren (this is 10 times his annual salary) and a $250,000 policy on Sarah (10 times her annual salary).
>
> Not completely satisfied with this recommendation, they consult another planner, who has them fill out a financial worksheet. After discussing their plans to put both children through four years of college, to keep the house, and to allow Sarah to stay home for 15 years if something happened to Loren, and after evaluating their current assets and debts, this planner recommends a $1 million policy for Loren and a $500,000 policy for Sarah.
>
> This makes more sense to them, given their hopes for the future and how they'd like to take care of each other if one dies first. They decide that they can afford to pay about $75 a month to buy the policies recommended by the second planner.

If You Have a Child With Special Needs

If you are the parent of a child with special needs, none of the methods above really captures what you need to do with insurance, which is to provide lifetime care for your child. You might want to buy much more life insurance than any of the models would ordinarily call for. And because your child's needs are not going to diminish with time, a permanent life insurance policy probably makes the most sense. A term policy might terminate just when you need it most, and renewing it when you're older is not going to be cheap.

Most disabled adults rely on government benefits, especially Medicaid, and inheriting a large insurance payment directly may jeopardize their eligibility for these benefits. Creating a special needs trust (see Chapter 3) is the best way to make sure that money you've left behind will be used to supplement government benefits, not interfere with them.

RESOURCES

More on special needs trusts. *Special Needs Trusts: Protect Your Child's Financial Future,* by Stephen Elias (Nolo), explains how these trusts work and how to use them as part of your estate plan.

How Much Life Insurance Costs

Of course, you can't figure out what you can afford without a sense of what these policies cost. They don't cost as much as you'd probably think. After all, the odds of dying young are, thankfully, low. Not surprisingly, the longer the term and the higher the benefit, the more the policy costs. If a life insurance company's going to insure you for 20 years, it will charge you more for the added risk. If the policy lasts only 10 years, it can charge you less because the company is taking less risk.

The sooner you buy a policy, the lower the rate will be for the entire term. Take a look at the table below, "The Older You Are, The More It Costs," and you'll see that a policy for a 45-year-old man costs close to three times as much as the same policy for a 30-year-old man. Life insurance rates also vary by where you live, what you do for a living, your health history, and the current financial markets.

Your Medical History

Your health history, of course, is a big deal to insurers. Their whole business model works only if the price of their policies accurately reflects the risk they're running to insure you. You're going to have to complete a health history for them, and they're going to either require that you have a basic medical exam or send a nurse to your house to do one. They'll also want to review your medical records. They'll want to know about your cholesterol level and blood pressure, as well as your age, your weight, and whether or not you smoke or used to. They'll want to know if you've ever taken blood pressure medicine or antidepressants.

Answering these questions truthfully and being honest about your health history is very important. Having less-than-perfect health doesn't mean you'll be denied coverage. But it may mean that you don't get the best rates the company offers. If you get a quote that you don't like, many companies will send you a letter explaining why you didn't get the best rate and encourage you to see your doctor to deal with any of the health issues they've raised. You might be able to negotiate a better rate by giving them more information or by taking a new medication. If you have a serious illness, say, diabetes; a previous heart attack; or cancer, you may need to work with insurance agents who specialize in finding coverage for people who are difficult to insure, and you will probably have to pay higher rates than others.

Not telling the whole truth during this approval process is definitely not a good idea. If an insurance company finds out that you lied about your health condition or your lifestyle (as in, you actually do smoke), it will cancel your policy or deny the benefits to your family.

It's also good to know that different companies have different rules on what they'll cover and at what cost. Once they've asked you enough questions, an insurance agent should be able to find several companies that will cover you, even though you've lived on planet Earth for a number of years with the accompanying effects on your health.

Getting Price Quotes

An insurance salesperson can get you quotes. Someone who is an agent for just one company, like Allstate or Farmer's Insurance, will get you quotes for that insurer's policies only. An independent insurance broker can get you quotes from many different companies. Only licensed insurance agents, whether they work for one company or broker several, can actually sell policies.

Many websites now offer automated quote services. Even though you still have to purchase a policy from a licensed agent, these sites are terrific for comparison shopping and often give referrals (or pass your contact information) to local agents. You type in your zip code and some basic health information about yourself and your family, select a coverage amount, and promptly get back quotes from many insurance companies.

Here's a few that I used to compare prices. All of my virtual shoppers lived in the same zip code and had excellent health—only their age and gender changed.

- www.insurance.com
- www.insweb.com
- www.selectquote.com
- www.Term4sale.com

Below are the results that I got for 10-, 15-, and 20-year term policies. Here's the executive summary: The longer the term, the more the policy costs.

The Longer the Term, the More It Costs			
Coverage	Term	35-year-old man (annual premium)	35-year-old woman (annual premium)
$1 million	10 years	$170-410	$130-350
$1 million	15 years	$310-525	$305-450
$1 million	20 years	$440-650	$400-570

Guess what? The older you are, the more term insurance costs. It is slightly more expensive for men than woman, and the price difference increases with age.

The Older You Are, The More It Costs			
Coverage Term	$500,000 20 years	$750,000 20 years	$1 million 20 years
30-year-old man	$255-355	$358-500	$440-614
30-year-old woman	$235-290	$323-410	$370-500
35-year-old man	$255-369	$358-523	$440-650
35-year-old woman	$235-325	$328-463	$400-570
45-year-old man	$635-810	$928-1,175	$1,200-1,500
45-year-old woman	$505-665	$862-1,190	$935-1,210

Agents and Brokers

There are two kinds of insurance agents: brokers, who represent many companies, and agents, who work for one company. Either one can do a good job for you, as long as they're willing to listen long enough to find out what you need from a policy. An ethical insurance agent won't sell you more of a policy than you need or sell you a whole life policy when term should do the trick (as it should for most families purchasing insurance for estate planning purposes).

Most insurance websites, like those I listed earlier, don't actually sell insurance themselves. They offer you quotes from hundreds of companies, all competing for your business. To actually buy a policy you have to work directly with an agent. You can do it online, but truthfully, a good agent is worth having a conversation with, even if it's just over the phone. Agents will probably ask you to consider a few things that you haven't yet, and they can be really helpful in identifying the right companies for you, based on your health history and lifestyle.

Insurance is a very competitive industry, and salespeople are compensated by the commissions on the policies they sell. Term policies don't generate big commissions, but ethical agents are happy to sell them to you, anyway. They reason that building up a relationship with you that's based on trust might lead to your purchase of other kinds of insurance (like homeowners or auto) or new referrals from families like yours.

Word of mouth is the best way to find the good agents. Every community has people who have been doing a good job for families for many years. Talk to your friends and neighbors. If you have a financial adviser, ask for a recommendation. And check with your local chamber of commerce and Rotary Club for referrals—insurance agents are often quite active in community organizations like that.

If you feel like you are getting strong-armed into buying more insurance than you need, just find a new agent and stick to your guns.

What to Ask Your Insurance Agent

✓ How is the insurance company rated by at least two of the major ratings services? (Rating services are discussed below.)

✓ Are the premiums guaranteed to stay the same for the entire policy period? Some policies don't guarantee this.

✓ After the term ends, can the policy be renewed? If so, what are the costs? Some policies will let you renew your coverage at the end of a term, but the premiums might go up.

✓ Is there a conversion period? Some policies let you convert a term policy to a whole life policy without having to get another medical exam. This can be a good thing if your health isn't as good as it once was and as a result you can't buy a similar policy anywhere else.

✓ Does it cost more if you pay the annual premium in monthly installments? Some companies charge you more if you don't pay annually.

Comparing Companies

When you're comparing policies, you also need to compare companies. After all, if you're getting into a 20-year deal with a company, you want to know that if you need it to pay out, it will still be in business and able to pay your benefit. All states regulate insurers who do business there; you can check with your state's agency (usually called a Department of Insurance, Division of Insurance, or Insurance Bureau) to see whether it has any information on the company you're considering.

There are companies that rate insurance companies, too. Here are four of the major ones:

- Weiss Ratings, www.weissratings.com, rates companies on the basis of their capital, investment safety, profitability, and stability. You have to purchase the reports.

- A.M. Best, www.ambest.com, offers an opinion on the relative financial strength and performance of the company, using letters from A++ to D. The site requires that you register, but the rating is free. The rating is clear and easy to understand.

- Moody's Investors' Services, www.moodys.com, rates a company's ability to meet its policyholder obligations and claims, using letters from Aaa to C. The site requires registration, and the information provided is detailed but not consumer-friendly.

- Standard and Poors, www.standardandpoors.com, rates each insurance company's ability to pay claims, using letters from AAA to CCC. You have to purchase the ratings.

You probably don't have to do this research yourself. When you get a quote from an insurance agent, make sure to ask for ratings from at least two of these companies for each insurance company you're considering. Don't buy a policy for anything but the most highly rated companies (for example, an AAA or AA from Standard and Poors), and get the agent to explain the ratings.

Naming Beneficiaries

Once you've decided on the policy you need and the death benefit you can afford, you've got one more big decision: whom to name as the beneficiary of your policy. Thankfully, this isn't usually complicated, but it does bear some thought.

When you buy a new policy, you name a primary beneficiary and a secondary (alternate) beneficiary. You do it on the enrollment forms that the company sends to you after it's approved your application for coverage. The primary beneficiary gets the money when you die. If that person dies before you do, or at the same time, the secondary beneficiary gets the money.

> **EXAMPLE:** Nelson bought a life insurance policy on his own life and named his wife Zelda as the primary beneficiary. He named his brother, Napoleon, as the secondary, or alternate, beneficiary. When Nelson and Zelda die together in a yachting accident, Napoleon receives the insurance proceeds.

If You've Been Divorced: Check Those Policies

If you've been married before, make extra sure to check all of your beneficiary designations.

If your divorce settlement agreement mandates that you name your ex-spouse as a beneficiary under an insurance policy for a certain number of years (a common practice), then you can't change that. If you are on good terms with your ex and raising minor children together, you might want to keep him or her as the beneficiary of your policy so that the children can be provided for.

But if you've simply forgotten to take your ex-spouse off the beneficiary form, your current spouse could be in for a nasty surprise if you die unexpectedly. Some states' laws automatically cancel beneficiary designations when you divorce, but others don't. My advice is not to rely on state law: Just review the designations on your life insurance policies and change them if they don't reflect your current wishes.

If you already own a policy but want to change your beneficiaries, ask the insurance carrier for a change of beneficiary form. Fill it out and send it back. Remember to keep a copy for your records.

Remember, it's really important to name the right people on these forms. Your will or trust has no effect on who gets your insurance proceeds. The beneficiary form that you fill out is what determines who inherits this money.

Here's how to fill out most forms.

Primary Beneficiaries:

- If you have a *will*, name your spouse or partner as the primary beneficiary. Your spouse will get the money directly. Example: "Madeline R. Reynoso, my spouse."

- If you have a *living trust*, name that trust as the primary beneficiary. It depends on the terms of the trust, but usually your spouse will have full access to the money. Whatever your spouse doesn't spend will stay in the trust, avoiding probate when that spouse dies, and be managed for your children if they're still young. Example: "The Johnson Family Trust, executed on January 4, 20xx."

Secondary Beneficiaries:

- If you have a *will* that creates a trust for your children, name that trust. Example: "the Rudolph Children's Trust, established by my will, executed on January 4, 20xx."

- If you have a *will* that doesn't create a trust for your children, name a custodian for them under the Uniform Transfers to Minors Act. Example: "Jane Smith, as custodian for Joseph Sherman, under the Arizona Uniform Transfers to Minors Act."

- If you have a *living trust,* you don't need to name a secondary beneficiary. Even after you pass away, your trust will continue to exist. It will be there to serve as the primary beneficiary. The money from your insurance policy will pass into the trust and go to the beneficiaries of the trust the way you decided it should be distributed when you created the trust.

EXAMPLE 1: Loren fills out the beneficiary form for his new life insurance policy by writing in Sarah as his primary beneficiary. For his secondary beneficiary, he writes "the Sanchez Family Trust, as established by my will, executed on December 4, 20xx." If Sarah is alive when Loren dies, she will receive the death benefit. If she dies before he does, or at the same time, the money will go to a trust established by Loren's will for the benefit of his children.

EXAMPLE 2: Ruth and Claudio Berner have a living trust. They purchase two term policies for $500,000 of coverage. On each policy they write in "the Berner Family Trust, created on November 15, 20xx," as the primary beneficiary. They don't list a secondary beneficiary because the trust will survive them. When either of them dies, the trust will receive the death benefit. All of the money will be available for the survivor's use. At the survivor's death, if there's any money left in the trust, it will pass to their children, in trust, and avoid probate.

Using Life Insurance to Reduce (and Pay) Federal Estate Tax

People with taxable estates (currently, only those with more than $2 million in assets) can use insurance benefits to pay their estate tax bill. This is done by transferring a life insurance policy to a separate trust. This trust is usually called an irrevocable life insurance trust, or ILIT.

The ILIT becomes the legal owner of your policy. It's okay for you to pay the premiums, but the whole thing works only if you don't have any legal control over the policy itself. After your death, the insurance benefit is paid to the ILIT. Because you didn't legally own the policy, none of the money it paid out is part of your taxable estate. The trustee of the insurance trust can then use the proceeds to purchase assets from your estate (real estate or a business, for example), and the money from the sale can be used to pay the estate tax. Many people purchase second-to-die insurance policies to fund these trusts.

This is high-end stuff. If you think it might make sense for you to set up an ILIT, see an estate planning attorney.

Name Beneficiaries for Bank
and Brokerage Accounts

∙∙

What you'll do here:

☐ Learn how to transfer bank accounts and securities directly to beneficiaries, without probate.

☐ Decide whether this strategy makes sense for you.

∙∙

Retirement accounts and life insurance aren't the only assets that pass to your family outside of your will or trust. You can also easily transfer bank accounts, stocks, mutual funds, and some government securities in the same way, simply by naming beneficiaries on the right forms. If you designate an account or investment as a "payable-on-death" (POD) or "transfer-on-death" (TOD) account, it will pass directly to the people you've named as beneficiaries, with no need for probate. And voilà—you've saved your family time, paperwork, and money.

Naming POD and TOD beneficiaries is a simple, inexpensive way to leave particular accounts to particular people. Used intelligently, this strategy can avoid the hassle and expense of probate and make transfers after death quick and easy. During your lifetime, the beneficiaries have no right to the money, and you can change your mind anytime you'd like about who should inherit the accounts.

For many young families, though, POD and TOD accounts aren't particularly important. Read through the examples below to see whether or not they might make sense for your family. If so, read on to find out the nuts and bolts of setting them up. If not, cross this task off your list and go on to the next chapter.

When POD and TOD Accounts Are a Good Idea—and When They're Not

Creating beneficiary designations for specific accounts is really great for certain things. If the only asset you own that might be subject to probate is a brokerage account or a bank account, using a POD account can help your family avoid probate without the time and expense of setting up a living trust.

EXAMPLE: Jack and Clara were priced out of the housing market in New York. They and their three children rent a flat in a nice part of town, waiting for the housing bubble to burst. Jack and Clara each have a 401(k) and life insurance policies. They have a joint savings and checking account at the bank for everyday expenses and a brokerage account where they've invested what they hope will be their down payment.

They consult an estate planner about the best way to avoid probate and plan for their kids. They think that they need a living trust. She advises them instead to make a will and make their bank accounts and brokerage accounts into POD or TOD accounts, naming a custodian to manage the money on behalf of the children. That way, none of their assets will pass through probate, their children's money will be managed, and they'll save $1,000 in lawyer's fees (a trust costs $1,000 more than a will to do where they live). She advises them to come back and make a living trust when they buy a house.

Naming a POD beneficiary can also be an excellent way for you to leave your separate accounts to your spouse or partner. That way, if you die first, your spouse will get immediate access to all of your cash and securities. But during your lifetime, the accounts will stay separate, and your spouse won't have any right to the assets in them.

EXAMPLE: Dan and his partner, Andrew, each have separate checking and savings accounts. They want to make sure that if either of them dies, the other will own the accounts. It is important to them to keep the accounts separate during their lifetimes. They fill out POD forms at their respective banks, naming each other as the beneficiary on the accounts. As a result, the accounts stay separately owned, but when one dies, the other will own the accounts and can use them to take care of their daughter, Kendra.

Beneficiary designations can also be a great way to leave a special account to a special person. If your parents, for example, gave you the down payment for a house or helped you buy a business, and you want to make sure that you pay them back upon your death, designating a brokerage or savings account for them is an easy way to make sure they're taken care of or to return their generosity. Or if you'd like to leave an account to a godchild or a sibling who needs extra help, you can do so by making them the beneficiary of that account.

EXAMPLE: Laura, a mother of two young children, wants to make sure that her mother would inherit her brokerage account if Laura dies first. She wants to make sure that her mother will always have enough money for adequate housing. She designates her mother as the beneficiary of that account and leaves everything else to her spouse in her will, naming her children as the alternate beneficiaries.

Good Uses for POD Accounts

You want to:

- Leave bank or brokerage accounts that you own separately to your spouse or partner.
- Leave an account to the guardian of your children as a gift.
- Leave extra cash to an adult child from a previous marriage.
- Leave a godchild a specific account.
- Leave a particular account to parents or a sibling.

As useful as they are, for most young families these tools are more like the extra tools on the Swiss army knife than the main blade. You shouldn't use them until after you've written a will or a trust. Why? Because you really need to name guardians for your kids, and only a will can do that.

Second, and probably more important, most young families worry most about what happens if *both* parents die. If you designate your spouse as the beneficiary of your accounts, but then you both die, the POD designation won't help. You usually can't name alternate, or secondary, beneficiaries for these accounts. That means that the accounts would be part of your estate, and your children wouldn't inherit them without a probate proceeding. The probate court would also need to appoint a property guardian to manage them.

Last, it's just easy to forget that you've designated certain accounts to certain people, and one important reason you're doing estate planning is to leave behind one integrated plan that manages all of your assets and treats your children equally. Beneficiary designations trump what your will says—whatever's on those beneficiary forms controls where the assets go after your death. (The only exception is in Washington state, which has a "superwill" law that says you can override beneficiary designations by referring to an account in your will.)

> **EXAMPLE:** Maria, who lives in Ohio, filled out a POD designation at her neighborhood bank, leaving her savings account, worth $25,000, to her son, Sam. At the time he was a struggling student at a culinary institute. She then forgot all about what she'd done and she never told Sam that she'd designated him as the beneficiary of that account.
>
> Later, Maria signed a will leaving everything she had equally to her four children: Sam, Mario, Kate, and Nick. A few years later Maria died. Kate was the executor. While figuring out what her mother had owned, she was informed by the savings and loan that the savings account, now worth $36,000, was payable only to Sam. By this time, Sam had a successful restaurant and didn't need the extra gift from his mother. But he got

the account. Everything else was split equally among all four siblings. Sam was under no obligation to even up the score, and he didn't.

What POD Accounts Aren't So Good For

They don't let you:

- Easily avoid probate, or manage children's assets, if both parents die.
- Name secondary (alternate) beneficiaries for accounts.
- Create an integrated estate plan for all of your assets.

How POD and TOD Accounts Work

A payable-on-death (POD) bank account is just a regular bank account that you leave to a particular person at your death. All you have to do is fill out some very simple paperwork at the bank designating a POD beneficiary for the account.

During your life, the beneficiary you name has no right to the money. If you change your mind about whom to leave the account to, you can just designate a different beneficiary on a new form from the bank. After your death, the named beneficiary owns the account. No probate is necessary to transfer the asset. Banks and credit unions offer these accounts. Some offer what's called a "Totten trust," which basically works the same way but is set up slightly differently: You open a bank account in your name "as trustee" for someone else.

> **EXAMPLE:** Odessa, who lives in New York, has a savings account with $14,000 in it. Odessa would like to leave the account to her niece, Stella, who is 19. Odessa fills out a payable-on-death form at her bank, naming Stella as the POD beneficiary on the account.

During Odessa's life, Stella has no right to the money in the account. When Odessa dies, Stella will own what's left, if anything, in the account. To claim it, she will need to go to the bank with a certified copy of Stella's death certificate and proper identification.

A transfer-on-death registration (TOD), like a POD bank account, lets you designate a beneficiary for stocks, bonds, and mutual funds in most states. As with a POD account, the beneficiary has no right to the assets while you're alive. After your death, the assets are transferred without probate, directly to the beneficiary.

If you own stocks or bonds, you probably hold them in a brokerage account (as opposed to having actual stock certificates in your possession). In that case, you'll get the paperwork from the financial institution holding your account. Every state but Louisiana and Texas has now adopted a law (the Uniform Transfer-on-Death Securities Registration Act) that permits TOD registration. (It's also sometimes called "beneficiary registration.")

If you own actual stock certificates (this is rare), you will have to get new certificates issued, showing that you own the stock in beneficiary form. Or you might consider transferring your stock to a brokerage account and naming a TOD beneficiary.

TIP

What to do if your state is behind the curve. Even if you live in Louisiana or Texas, you may be able to register your stocks as TOD—if either the stock owner or the stock issuer has any connection to a state that has passed the law, TOD registration is available.

Unfortunately, just because TOD registration is allowed almost everywhere doesn't mean that your broker will offer it. The law doesn't require them to do so—it just gives them the option. If you can't get your broker to cooperate, you can always move your account to one that does.

EXAMPLE: Harriet owns a brokerage account that holds mutual funds. Upon her death, she would like to leave it to her nephew, Franklin, who is 21. She contacts her brokerage firm and asks for a transfer-on-death registration form. They tell her that they don't offer TOD accounts. She moves her account to another brokerage house that does allow TOD accounts. She then designates Franklin as the TOD beneficiary of the account. Upon her death, Franklin will be the new owner of the account, after presenting the new brokerage company with a certified copy of Harriet's death certificate and proper identification.

Warning: Creditors and Taxes Get Paid First

Naming a beneficiary for your bank or stock accounts doesn't change a thing when it comes to the rights of creditors or the IRS. It's true that you've designated a new owner, but your executor is going to have to pay your estate's outstanding debts or expenses. If necessary, the POD beneficiaries may have to chip in.

Though most families aren't subject to the estate tax at this point, anyone who dies with more than $2 million will owe some, and TOD and POD accounts count toward that total. If your estate owes debts or taxes, or if your immediate family members need the money to support themselves after your death, these accounts can also be used to pay the bills. Neither scenario is likely to happen, but it's important to know that these accounts are part of your estate.

FDIC Insurance

POD accounts offer an unexpected benefit: They let you cover more money under the federal government's insurance program (FDIC) for bank accounts than an individual account does. Normally, you can insure up to a total of $100,000 at one bank. But if you name POD beneficiaries, you can insure up to $100,000 for each "qualifying" beneficiary. Which beneficiaries qualify? Under the FDIC's rules, your spouse, child, grandchild, parent, or sibling counts.

EXAMPLE: Steven has a savings account worth $210,000. He designates his parents, Tom and Jane, as the payable-on-death beneficiaries of that account. Because both of them are qualifying beneficiaries, $200,000 of that savings account is covered by FDIC insurance. If Steven hadn't designated anyone as a payable-on-death beneficiary, only $100,000 of the account would be covered by that insurance.

How to Set Up a POD or TOD Account

To add a POD or TOD designation to an asset, you need to fill out the institution's paperwork. Here are the most important things to keep in mind as you fill in the forms.

Joint Accounts With Rights of Survivorship

If you and your spouse or partner have an account together, you can name a POD or TOD beneficiary for it as long as you own the account with a right of survivorship. That's the most common way for two people to own bank and stock accounts together. On your account statement it will usually say something like "Bob and Tina Garcia, JT WROS," which stands for "joint tenants with right of survivorship." Or it might say you own it as "tenants by the entirety," which is like joint tenancy but is available in only about half the states and only to married couples or registered domestic partners.

If a joint account has the right of survivorship, it means that when one of you dies, the survivor will own the whole account automatically. A POD or a TOD designation will apply only after the death of the surviving owner.

EXAMPLE: Bob and Shirley own a mutual fund account as joint tenants. They name Bob's son from a previous marriage, Robert, as the TOD beneficiary on the account. Robert will own the account only after both Bob and Shirley have died.

Because an account owner can always change POD beneficiary designations, the surviving owner can change the POD or TOD beneficiary.

EXAMPLE: Back to Bob and Shirley. After Bob dies, Shirley and Robert have a terrible falling-out. Shirley changes the TOD beneficiary of the account to her goddaughter Shelly. Robert inherits nothing at Shirley's death four years later.

If you are concerned about the surviving owner changing your beneficiary designations, you can create your own separate account and name your own beneficiary. If you are married, though, you'll probably need to get your spouse's consent for this. (See "If You're Married: Spouses' Rights," below.)

Joint Accounts Without the Right of Survivorship

If you own an account with someone else but don't have a right of survivorship, you can't set up a POD or TOD designation. Each owner has the right to leave half of the account to anyone that he or she chooses to leave it do, by will or trust. That's not likely something that you'd have, though. In my experience, married couples either keep their accounts separate or own them together with the right of survivorship. (For the details, see Chapter 2.)

If You're Married: Spouses' Rights

Married couples (and in some states, registered domestic partners) are bound by state law to provide fairly for each other. Most married couples leave everything to each other first, anyway, so this isn't likely to be an issue for you. But every once in a while, a married person wants to designate someone else as the POD beneficiary of a specific account. There's nothing wrong with doing that, but you should first get your spouse's written consent. If you don't get that consent, your spouse could undo that transfer after your death.

If you live in a community property state, then even if the account is in your name only, if it contains money you earned during the marriage, that money (and the interest it earns) is community property, owned equally by each spouse. Only a separate written agreement can change this. So if you don't get your spouse's consent, and you don't have a property agreement, your spouse could claim half the money in the account at your death.

If you live in a non-community property state, a surviving spouse who doesn't like what you've left him or her could claim a percentage of your property. State laws vary, but a spouse is commonly entitled to about a third of what the deceased spouse owned. Assets in a POD bank account or TOD stock account may or may not be subject to such a claim; it depends on state law.

Community and Non-Community Property States		
Community Property States		**Non-Community Property States**
Alaska*	Nevada	All the rest.
Arizona	New Mexico	
California	Texas	
Idaho	Washington	
Louisiana	Wisconsin	
* Only if spouses sign a community property agreement		

There's usually a place at the bottom of beneficiary forms for a spouse to sign, documenting his or her consent to the beneficiary designation. If there isn't, you can write up something saying that you and your spouse have agreed to the beneficiary designation. Your spouse should sign it in front of a notary.

EXAMPLE: Marco, who lives in Arizona, wants to designate a POD beneficiary for a bank account that's in his name alone. He wants to leave a special gift to his nephew, Josh, who's a struggling artist. Because he lives in a community property state, he needs to get his wife to consent to that beneficiary designation on the bank's form. At the bottom of the form, it says:

> SPOUSAL CONSENT (for use in community property states): This section must be signed and dated by the spouse of an individual Account Owner, and the spouse's signature notarized, if the Account Owner is designating a primary beneficiary other than his/her spouse.
>
> I, the undersigned spouse of the Account Owner named above, hereby consent to and accept the beneficiary designation without regard to whether I survive or predecease my spouse.

(Then there's a place for the spouse and the notary to sign.)

Naming Multiple Beneficiaries

If you name more than one person as a POD or TOD beneficiary, all the beneficiaries will receive an equal share of what's in the account upon your death. That's fine, of course, as long as that's what you want to do with your account. But if it's not, you'll have to either open up new accounts or use a will or living trust to distribute your assets as you'd like.

EXAMPLE: Carol leaves her savings account POD to her three children and her two cousins. At Carol's death, the account will be split equally into five shares.

If you want to leave unequal shares in a POD bank account to each beneficiary, check with your bank—some states don't allow it. You can work around this rule by opening up separate, unequal accounts and leaving one to each beneficiary—but that's a lot of hassle.

If you want to leave unequal shares of a TOD stock account to different beneficiaries, you can do so if the stockbroker or transfer agent allows it. If you do, make sure that the percentages you list add up to 100%. Financial institutions won't know what to do if there's anything left over, even a fraction of a cent.

> **EXAMPLE:** Kyle wants to leave his four nieces and nephews his brokerage account as TOD beneficiaries. He writes each of them down on the beneficiary form and writes "25%" next to each name.

Naming Children

If you are leaving an account worth more than a few thousand dollars to a minor child, you should leave it in the care of a custodian until the child is at least 21, older if your state allows it. (See Chapter 3.) If you want to leave a POD or TOD account to adult children, of course, there's no problem.

> **EXAMPLE:** Terry and Robin, who live in Georgia, want to leave some money to their young goddaughter Lisa. So they name as the TOD beneficiary for their mutual fund account, Lisa's mother, Carol Ann Jones, "as the custodian for Lisa Jane Jones, under the Georgia Uniform Transfers to Minors Act, until she reaches the age of 21."

Naming Alternate Beneficiaries

One big drawback to POD and TOD accounts is that they're not as flexible as a will or a trust. You can't usually name alternate beneficiaries to inherit the account if the first person you've named dies before you do. So, if the beneficiaries you've named on your POD or TOD paperwork die before you do, you should update your designations. If you don't, and one or more of the beneficiaries has died before you, the surviving ones will inherit the account.

If there are no surviving beneficiaries, the account will go to your estate. Under the terms of most wills, the account will then pass to the "residuary" beneficiary of your will: the person who gets everything that isn't left to other named beneficiaries. Depending on the size of your estate, this could also mean that the account will be subject to probate before it can be transferred to the person who inherits it.

> **EXAMPLE:** Peter and Harriet name each other as the POD beneficiaries of their brokerage accounts. They aren't married and don't own a house—it seems like a simple way to take care of each other if one died first. Years later, both die together. Their young children are the beneficiaries under the wills that Peter and Harriet had written. Because the two brokerage accounts are worth $120,000 each, they must be probated before they can be transferred to the trust that is established for the children by the wills.

Government Bonds and Notes

You can also name TOD beneficiaries for government securities like Treasury bills and notes and savings bonds. To do this, you register the security in your name, followed by the words "payable on death to _____." If you want to leave the security to a child, name a custodian to manage the money until the child is an adult. You can name only one primary owner and one beneficiary. Go to www.treasurydirect.gov to get more information on how to set up transfer-on-death registration for government bonds and notes.

RESOURCES

More information on POD and TOD designations. See *8 Ways to Avoid Probate,* by Mary Randolph (Nolo).

Avoiding Probate of Your House: Transfer-on-Death Deeds

Arizona	Kansas	Nevada	Ohio
Arkansas	Missouri	New Mexico	Wisconsin
Colorado			

If you want to transfer your house to someone without going through probate, for most people the only option is placing that house into a living trust. But in the states listed here you can now use transfer-on-death deeds (also called beneficiary deeds) to leave real estate to someone else, instead. Like POD and TOD accounts, these deeds allow for the quick transfer of property to one or more beneficiaries. During your lifetime, the beneficiaries have no right to the property.

This can be a terrific option for some people, but not usually for those with young children. If you want to leave your house to minors, you're better off using a trust to avoid probate. This makes it possible for the trustee to either sell the house and use the money for the children's benefit or maintain the house for them to live in. It also gets around the difficulty of having multiple owners of one piece of property—if everyone can't agree on what to do with it, it will have to be sold and the proceeds divided.

Create Health Care Directives and a Power of Attorney for Finances

What you'll do here:

☐ Consider your choices for medical care.

☐ Choose an agent for health care.

☐ Choose an agent for financial matters.

☐ Find out where to get the proper forms for your state.

I f you died unexpectedly, your family would rely on your will or your living trust to put things in order and pass along your property to the right people. But if you became seriously ill or were injured, those documents wouldn't do them any good. They would need documents that gave them the legal authority to act on your behalf.

Two legal documents accomplish this:

- **A health care directive** allows you to name an agent to act on your behalf with respect to medical decisions. If you could no longer communicate with your doctors, your agent would speak for you and manage your care. You may also state your wishes for end-of-life care, to direct your doctors and your agent.

- **A durable power of attorney for finances** lets you name someone to manage your finances if someday you couldn't.

Do young, healthy people like you need these documents? Yes. After all, anyone can be injured in a car accident or require hospitalization unexpectedly. If you're unable to manage your daily affairs or communicate with your doctors, your family will rely on these documents to do both. And at the end of life, they provide a clear statement of your wishes concerning treatment—keeping this agonizing decision within your family and out of court.

If you don't create these documents before you're unable to manage your own affairs, your family will have to go to court and ask to be appointed as your conservator or guardian. That's the only way that they can step in and manage things on your behalf. This is expensive and public—and unnecessary if you get the job done now.

> **EXAMPLE:** Sergio, a young father of three, was in a tragic motorcycle accident one rainy night. Like most people, he'd never completed a health care directive or a power of attorney for finances. He suffered severe brain damage in the accident and faced a long period of recovery and an uncertain future. Although he was able to physically sign documents that were placed in front of him, he couldn't understand what he was signing or why his family needed to have the power to make medical and financial decisions on his behalf.
>
> Clara, his wife, asked an attorney to draft health care directives and a power of attorney for finances for Sergio. The attorney told Clara that it was too late for Sergio to sign such documents and that she'd have to ask a court to be named Sergio's conservator instead.

Health Care Directives

Your right to control your medical treatment comes from the U.S. Constitution. In 1990, the United States Supreme Court ruled that if you state your wishes about end-of-life treatment in a clear and convincing way, your wishes should be respected by hospitals, physicians, and family members. This is sometimes called a con- stitutional "right to die," free of government intrusion into the intimate matter of how and when one's life should end. Every state now provides health care directive forms that you can use to state your medical wishes and name a health care agent.

States use different names for their health care forms and how they're structured. I'll refer to them as your "health care directives."

No matter what your states calls these forms, all of them allow you to direct your care and name a health care agent.

The majority of states provide two health care documents:

- one in which you state your wishes regarding the use of life-sustaining medical treatment, often called a living will, and
- one in which you designate a health care agent or proxy, often called a durable power of attorney for health care.

The rest of the states combine both documents into one, usually called an advance health care directive.

It's not hard to find health care directives for your state. They are widely available, usually for free, and they are easy to fill out and make legally valid. (See "Where to Get Your State's Forms and More Information," below.) The federal government requires every facility that receives Medicare or Medicaid to provide information about health care directives to newly admitted patients and to record a patient's health care directives as part of their medical records.

What Health Care Directives Do

✓ Appoint someone to make decisions for you if you can't communicate for yourself.

✓ Name the doctor that you'd like to supervise your care.

✓ State whether or not you'd like to receive end-of-life medical treatments that would prolong your life artificially, such as artificial respiration or nutrition.

✓ State your wishes for relief from pain medications or other aspects of your medical or personal care.

✓ State your wishes for organ donation after death.

You absolutely don't need an attorney to create your health care directives. If you're working with a lawyer to draft an estate plan, though, these documents should be created for you as part of that plan.

Your Living Will

Making your health care directives require you to make some decisions about what medical treatments you would, or wouldn't, want if you were unable to speak for yourself. This part of your health care directives is often called a living will.

You have the right to state your wishes concerning medical treatment that serves only to prolong your life by artificial means. This is often called life-sustaining treatment. To put it another way, you have the right to choose to die by declining certain kinds of health care at the end of your life. If you want all medical procedures used to prolong your life as long as it is medically possible to do so, you can say that in your living will instead.

You've probably given little thought before to this issue, but don't be intimidated. First, most state forms provide default choices that you can select if they are close to what you'd want. Second, there are excellent resources available to you on the Internet and in books if you want to educate yourself before making a decision. (See "Where to Get Your State's Forms and More Information," below.) Third, because your right to make such choices comes from the U.S. Constitution, you're not limited to the forms prepared by your state legislature. If there's something you feel strongly about, you can attach your own statement of medical wishes to the form you're using and ask that these wishes be respected.

Before you fill out a health care directive, here are some things to consider:

- If you become terminally ill, would you like doctors to treat you as long as it is medically possible to do so?
- Are there certain treatments that you would want to receive?
- Are there certain treatments that you would not want to receive?
- If you could not eat or drink independently, would you want doctors to give you nutrients and water through a feeding tube?

- If you could not breathe independently, would you want doctors to use respirators to prolong your life?
- Would you want to be kept as pain-free and comfortable as possible during a final illness?

EXAMPLE: Lucy, a resident of North Carolina, wants to put together her health care directives. She will use a North Carolina Health Care Power of Attorney to name her health care agent and an alternate agent. She will use the North Carolina Declaration of a Desire for a Natural Death to state her end-of-life choices. In it, she states that she does not want her life to be prolonged by extraordinary means or by artificial nutrition or hydration if someday her doctors determine that her condition is terminal and incurable or if she is in a persistent vegetative state.

She may also attach her own additional directions to this form, such as her statement that she wishes to die in her home, surrounded by her friends and family, and to receive all available relief from pain and discomfort. She will sign it in front of two witnesses.

Making End-of-Life Choices

Often people I work with get a bit giddy when we get to this part of the planning process and make jokes about "pulling the plug." Others get very serious and worry that requesting no life-sustaining measures now might rob them of the chance to take advantage of future medical advances. Occasionally I meet someone who is most concerned with draining the family's resources unnecessarily. Some people I've worked with just want to skip these documents and let their spouse or their children decide what to do if it's ever necessary.

If that last option is the most appealing, take a deep breath and try to imagine your family having to make an agonizing decision about whether or not to continue life-sustaining medical treatment for you. Imagine how much better they would feel knowing that you took the time to tell them what you'd like them to do. And if your family can't agree, your doctors will have written evidence of what you would have wanted and will be bound to follow these wishes. The tragic cases that make the news, and sometimes the courts, are almost always situations in which a person left nothing in writing. That means it's left to state law and the courts to determine who, if anyone, is authorized to make the toughest end-of-life decisions.

It might help to remember that your end-of-life instructions apply only when medical treatments may prolong your life for a limited amount of time but not help you recover, and when *not* receiving treatment will lead to your death. Doctors, usually two of them, have to determine whether or not you are at this point.

Choosing to forgo life-sustaining treatments doesn't mean that your doctors won't ease your pain or try to make you comfortable in other ways. This is called "palliative care." Those who administer it focus on providing a patient with dignity and comfort, not in trying to cure a disease or prolong life just because it is medically possible to do so. Not all doctors have been trained in palliative care, but it is getting increased attention from the medical community, and it is worth discussing with your doctor and your agent if it is important to you. You may receive palliative care at home, in a hospital, or at a hospice.

Finally, you might find it comforting to know that choosing to forgo life-sustaining treatment doesn't affect your medical treatment at all when you are in a non-life-threatening situation.

Doctors who receive a properly signed and witnessed or notarized statement of your wishes for medical treatment are legally bound to honor your wishes or transfer you to the care of another physician who will honor them. At least this is true in theory. At some hospitals your agent might have to fight hard to get your wishes honored—all the more reason to choose someone who would be a strong advocate.

In some states, your right to refuse life-sustaining treatment is limited if you are pregnant. You can go ahead and state your wishes; if your health care directives were needed and you were pregnant, the possibility of saving the fetus would be factored into treatment decisions.

> ## What's a DNR?
>
> A do-not-resuscitate or DNR order is different from a living will or health care directive. It is a simple form that you can use to tell emergency medical personnel that you don't want to receive cardiopulmonary resuscitation (CPR) if there's a medical emergency. CPR is used to restart your heart and get you breathing again.

Your Health Care Agent's Duties

A durable power of attorney for health care allows you to designate an agent to act on your behalf. This person is sometimes referred to as a proxy, surrogate, representative, or attorney-in-fact. No matter what the job title, this person's job is to act in your best interests and make the decisions required for your health care. You should name alternate agents in case your first choice is unwilling or unable to act for you.

As long as you can understand and communicate in some way, your decisions will be the ones that doctors respect. Your agent will act on your behalf only if you are unable to make your own health care decisions. This could be because you are unconscious or because you are no longer able to make decisions. States differ tremendously on how a patient is determined to be in this state and on who should make this decision and document it—but typically two doctors, one of whom is your attending physician, must agree.

In addition to naming an agent, you can, in your durable power of attorney for health care, define how much authority your agent may have over such things as medical care or services, the choice of doctors treating you, and the release of confidential medical information about you. States differ on an agent's authority, but typically, your agent has these rights unless you choose to limit them:

- to consent or refuse to consent to any medical treatment.

- to select or discharge health care providers and institutions.

- to approve or disapprove diagnostic tests and surgical procedures.

- to direct that life-sustaining treatment or procedures be used, withheld, or withdrawn, and

- to authorize anatomical gifts or autopsy, and in some states to direct for the disposition of remains.

Picking Your Agent

Obviously, picking the right person to serve as your health care agent is critically important. You're giving this person broad powers to act if someday you're no longer able to act for yourself. You are truly putting your life in his or her hands. Most people choose their spouses, but you are not required to do so.

State law varies a bit on who can serve as your agent, but generally your agent:

- must be at least 18 years old

- cannot be your health care provider or the owner or operator of a care facility (unless the person is also your spouse or close relative), and

- cannot be an employee of a health care provider (unless the person is also your spouse or close relative).

When trying to choose an agent, here are some things you should ask yourself:

- Would my agent be a good advocate for me?

- Does my agent really know what I would want?

- Would my agent respect my wishes?

- Could my agent be with me in the hospital?

- What would my agent do if family members disagreed with my wishes?

Like picking a guardian, there's no magic way to find the best person for the job. I've had clients pick close friends who are health care professionals, in the hopes that they'll best be able to advocate for them. I've had clients specifically NOT pick their parents, because they felt that their parents would simply not respect their written wishes but would substitute their own. I've had clients choose their adult children, and others who want to shield those children from this burden and responsibility. The right person for you is the person who you feel is best able to act on your behalf and to carry out your wishes.

You should always try to pick one agent and one alternate. I wouldn't recommend choosing two people to serve together. If you give two people equal authority as your agents and they disagree over what to do, the whole point of your planning will be defeated. If you're not sure whom to pick and are worried about offending someone, talk to everyone and see if together you can come up with someone to serve as the agent and another as alternate.

> **EXAMPLE:** Julia, a single mother, struggled with whether to pick her younger sister, Ilana, or her older sister, Hannah, as her health care agent. She was close to both of them and didn't want to offend either of them. Over the holidays, the three sisters discussed Julia's concerns and decided that because Ilana lived much closer to Julia, she was Julia's best first choice. Hannah agreed to serve as her alternate choice, just in case Ilana couldn't do it.

After You've Picked Someone: Time to Talk

Once you've decided whom to pick, make sure that the person knows it. You don't want your agent to be surprised by the job—the very best thing you can do is sit down now and discuss your health care wishes and concerns.

The more your agent knows about what you would or wouldn't want, the better job they'll be able to do for you. Filling out your health care directives is a good first step, but having a serious discussion about your values, goals, and concerns about medical treatment is really important, too.

It's not always easy to have that kind of a discussion with a close friend or family member, but it's at least as important as the legal document you'll end up with. No document, no matter how detailed, can capture the dimensions of what you care about, what you're worried about, what you're willing to tolerate, and what you just couldn't live with. Talking about these things now can avoid misunderstandings later.

You'll also want to make sure that your agents have a copy of your properly signed health care directives and easy access to the originals. They'll need them should you become incapacitated.

> **EXAMPLE:** Peter, a single parent, names his brother Tyson to serve as his health care agent. He names his sister-in-law Mary as his alternate agent, in case Tyson is unable to serve as his health care agent.
>
> If Peter were to become ill, he would of course be in charge of discussing his condition with his doctors and making decisions about what to do. If Peter should become unable to communicate, though, it would be Tyson's job to make health care decisions on his behalf. Mary would be the backup agent.
>
> Peter, Tyson, and Mary discuss Peter's concerns about treatment, and Peter gives Tyson and Mary a copy of his health care directives. He also tells them that he has the original in a fire-proof box in his office and tells them the combination to the box.

Where to Get Your State's Forms and More Information

You can get health care directives at hospitals, nursing homes, and senior centers, and from your doctor. There are also excellent resources on the Internet if you want more guidance on how to approach health care directives and state-specific forms. Here are three of my favorites:

www.compassionandchoices.org. This organization educates and advocates for choice and care at the end of life. You can download a health care directive for any state, and each comes with helpful questions about your goals for medical treatment and your values.

www.caringinfo.org. This is the website of the National Hospice and Palliative Care Organization. You can download health care directives for every state, and they do an excellent job at helping you work through your health care concerns and values.

www.agingwithdignity.org. Aging With Dignity is an organization that has developed Five Wishes, an advance directive that they say meets the legal requirements of 39 states and the District of Columbia. Even if you end up using your state's specific forms, the Five Wishes form can be a great starting place for working through your feelings about end-of-life care and beginning a discussion about these issues with your family and friends.

Also helpful are these sites:

www.growthhouse.org. This site has terrific resources for life-threatening illness and end-of-life care, including the *Handbook for Mortals*, a book that you can read online that has a lot of useful information on end-of-life choices.

www.ama-assn.org/ama/pub/category/7630.html. This is part of the American Medical Assocation's website. You can find your state's medical association's website on this list. Each state's medical association will have state-specific forms and information on health care directives.

 RESOURCES

Quicken WillMaker Plus (Nolo) can, in addition to creating wills and trusts, generate health care directives for all states except Louisiana.

California residents can also use *Living Wills & Powers of Attorney for California*, by Shae Irving (Nolo), to create their own advance health care directives.

Making It Legal

Each state has its own rules for how you must sign your health care directives for them to be legally binding. Most require you to sign them in front of at least two witnesses. Some require, or allow, you to sign in the presence of a notary public. These signing directions should be clearly spelled out on your state's form. Pay attention to them—if you don't, your document could be invalid.

After you sign, make copies and give them to your designated agents, your family, your doctor, and any hospital in which you are likely to receive treatment.

Changing Your Mind

You can revoke your health care directives at any time. In most states, little legal formality is required. You can simply rip up your existing document and make a new one. You should, of course, also notify your agent and your doctor that your old documents have been changed. Make sure that all copies of your old documents have been destroyed.

I think the safest thing is to sign a formal revocation of your old document, just to document that you no longer want it ever to take effect. This can be a simple written statement that you are revoking the document that you signed on a particular date. Sign it in front of two witnesses or a notary public. Then make a new one.

Durable Powers of Attorney for Finances

A durable power of attorney for finances is another document that you should have as part of your estate plan. It authorizes your agent to act for you with respect to money and property. So, if you were in the hospital for a few weeks, your agent could pay your bills, clean your house, manage your investments, and make other financial decisions on your behalf. Without a durable power of attorney, your family would run into a brick wall when they attempted to act on your behalf.

If you look at it from the point of view of a bank or insurance company, it all makes sense. Imagine that your brother needs to use your money to pay your medical bills. He can't sign your checks. And if he asks your bank to deliver $1,500 from your checking account, the bank won't do it without something proving that your brother is authorized to act for you. After all, they don't know he isn't trying to steal your money to go to Las Vegas.

A durable power of attorney for finances gives institutions the assurance that they need to work with someone who's acting for you. If you don't take the time to create one while you're competent to do so, the only alternative your family will have is to go to court and ask that someone be named your conservator—which is expensive, restrictive, and public.

Some couples have joint checking accounts. If so, your spouse or your partner could still write checks for you if necessary. But that's not a substitute for having a durable power of attorney in place as well. Couples who travel together can both be injured at the same time, and they need to name backup agents to take care of money and property in that case. Couples who own property separately need a durable power of attorney for finances to allow each other to act with respect to it. And married couples don't have unlimited rights to deal with property that's owned jointly—without a power of attorney, one spouse can't sell property or cars without the consent of the other.

Finally, when someone is ill, there's more to deal with than just writing checks. Sometimes stock or other property must be sold, houses or apartments must be cleaned up or vacated, or nursing homes must be found and paid for. To do any of those things you need the authority granted by a durable power of attorney for finances.

> ### But I Have a Trust!
>
> If your estate plan includes a living trust, and the trust holds your property to avoid probate, it's true that you're ahead of the game. Your "successor trustee," the person you named in your trust to take over management of the assets someday, can step in. But you still need a durable power of attorney so that someone can manage the property that's outside of the trust, such as small bank accounts, your life insurance polices, and your retirement accounts. Your power of attorney can even authorize your agent to transfer property into your trust, which can make a huge difference to families who need to do last-minute estate planning when someone's terminally ill.

What Your Agent Can Do

You have control over what powers your agent has. These can be quite broad or very narrow—it's up to you. When you're creating a durable power of attorney as part of a comprehensive estate plan, the broader the powers you grant, the better. You want your agent to be able to take whatever action is necessary if you're unable to act for yourself.

Using most durable power of attorney forms, you can give your agent authority over some or all of these things:

- using your assets to pay your everyday expenses
- handling transactions with banks and other financial institutions
- buying, selling, maintaining, and paying debts and taxes on property
- filing and paying your taxes
- managing your retirement accounts
- collecting government benefits owed to you
- investing your money in financial markets
- buying and selling insurance policies for you

- operating your small business
- making gifts on your behalf
- transferring your property to a living trust that you've already set up
- filing legal actions on your behalf, and
- paying for your personal care and supporting your family.

In using the authority you've granted, your agent must act only in your best interest and never for personal benefit. The agent must keep careful records and never mix your assets with anyone else's. Your agent must avoid conflicts of interest, such as purchasing your property for his or her own use, unless your durable power of attorney specifically grants the right to do so.

The power of attorney that you sign will state when and how your agent can be liable for breaking the rules. Generally, an agent who acts badly on purpose can be liable to repay the economic harm that results. But your agent is not liable for ordinary acts that don't work out well—say, an investment in a credible company that didn't do as well as expected.

When a Power of Attorney Takes Effect

You have a choice about when your agent's authority takes effect. You can give your agent power to act as soon as you sign the documents or specify that your agent's authority will begin only if you're incapacitated.

Most powers of attorney created by young, healthy folks like you are written so that they take effect only if someday you are no longer able to manage your own affairs. That way, as long as you are healthy and capable, you retain complete control over your property. This is often called a "springing" power of attorney, because it springs into effect only if you become incapacitated.

Proving incapacity usually requires that at least one doctor sign a statement stating that you are unable to manage your own affairs. This isn't a problem for someone facing major surgery, but it can be a problem for families when someone they love is facing a long-term degenerative disease, like dementia. In such situations, families can disagree about whether or not someone is incapable of managing daily affairs, and it is difficult to use a springing power of attorney to help.

It can also be a problem because federal law makes doctors liable for giving out confidential health care information without a patient's consent. This can create a chicken-and-egg problem: An agent needs medical information (a doctor's statement of incapacity) to take charge under a durable power of attorney, but the doctor can't give that information without a patient's consent, and the patient either can't or won't give it.

For this reason, most estate planners get their clients to sign a consent form for the release of medical information along with a durable power of attorney for finances. Another way to avoid both issues is to make your power of attorney effective as soon as you sign it. That way, your agent will have immediate power to act for you, and no doctor will have to determine your capabilities or lack of them.

There's nothing wrong with a power of attorney that's in effect right away, but because these documents give others so much power, I'd recommend their use only sparingly, especially when you're young and healthy. Of course, if you don't trust your agent, maybe you should choose someone else.

TIP

Get an institution's own form. If you deal heavily with one institution, such as a bank or a brokerage firm, ask if it has its own, in-house power of attorney form, just for the assets that it holds for you. Even though institutions are legally required to accept valid powers of attorney, I've found that it never hurts to fill out theirs, too. It can make things a lot easier in a crisis.

Whom Should You Choose as an Agent?

For obvious reasons, it's very important that your agent is someone whom you trust completely. You are giving this person a blank check and the power to sign it. Often spouses choose each other as a first choice. That's usually the best idea: Otherwise, you'll run the risk that the healthy spouse could struggle with the ill spouse's agent for control over jointly held assets. For a second choice, people often choose the same person that they've already chosen as a second-choice trustee or executor.

You can name two people to serve jointly, but that will require them to agree on every action that they take on your behalf. That can be cumbersome at the least or lead to a lawsuit at the worst. You can give them the authority to act separately, but that creates problems, too. Really, as with your health care directives, it's probably best to choose just one person to act for you. If you're worried about how your family will feel, talk with them about it, and see whether you can all agree on what would work best.

Most agents serve without compensation, though they can be reimbursed for any expenses that they pay on your behalf. You can, however, provide (in the document) for payment.

Whomever you choose, discuss your decision with family members—and, of course, the person you've chosen—before you sign the document. If you think your family will object to your choice, that's an even better reason to let them know about it in advance. The Busy Family's Toolkit contains a place for you to record your choices. (See "My Agent for Financial Management.")

Making It Legal

You should sign your durable power of attorney in front of a notary public. (This is required in all states but California. California residents can choose to have their forms witnessed or notarized, but most financial institutions prefer notarized forms.)

Some states require the agent to also sign the form. Some states require you to file your durable power of attorney with your county's land record office. Your state's forms will have instructions on the proper way to sign them and whether or not to record them in your county. Make sure to follow the specific instructions, or your form won't be valid. If you have questions about what to do, check with a local senior center or bank; they can often help.

Once you've signed your form, make sure that your agents have a copy of the signed document and know where to find your original in case they ever need to find it.

Where to Get Your State's Forms

You can find durable power of attorney forms for finances in many of the same places that have the forms for health care: senior centers, state government offices that work with the elderly, and financial institutions. For some reason, though, they aren't as easy to find on the Internet as health care directives are. The best source of forms is Quicken WillMaker Plus—using its simple question-and-answer format, you can easily create powers of attorney for every state except Louisiana. States usually have a standard form, called a statutory form, that's available through the state attorney's general office.

RESOURCES

Quicken WillMaker Plus (Nolo) can, in addition to creating wills and trusts, generate powers of attorney for finances for all states except Louisiana.

Changing Your Mind

You can always revoke your power of attorney. You can sign a document that's called a Notice of Revocation, or you can destroy all the copies and the original of the existing documents. It's always safer to do both, really. That way, your intent will be clear to everyone, and you won't worry that somewhere someone has the old version. If you recorded the original document with your county, make sure to file the revocation as well. If you used Quicken WillMaker Plus to make your power of attorney, you can use it to easily create a revocation form. If you used a form that you got somewhere else, you might have a hard time finding a revocation form. You can just write down your intent to revoke the power of attorney and sign it in front of two witnesses or a notary public.

TIP

Don't leave your ex-spouse in charge. If you get divorced, make sure to update your power of attorney. In some, but not all, states your ex-spouse's authority is automatically revoked by divorce. Don't rely on state law. Just update your documents.

Keep Your Plan Safe and Up to Date

Congratulations! You've now completed an estate plan for your family, or at least worked through virtually every issue that you'll need to be able to complete one with an estate planner. But before we get into the nitty-gritty of what to do next, stop.

Take a minute and realize what a gift you've given those you love. Even though you hope that none of the hard work you done will ever *really* matter, you can rest assured that if it does, your family will really appreciate the time you've taken, and the care you've taken, to make sure that they're well provided for.

You've done something that most people haven't: You've made an estate plan. By doing so, you've made sure that you, not a probate judge, are in charge of the difficult decisions. You've also made sure that your family will inherit your assets as easily and as efficiently as possible. I hope you feel good.

What You've Accomplished

By working through this book, you've:

- made a complete inventory of what your family owns
- planned for your children, so that if you die before they grow up, they'll be raised by people you love and respect
- managed your children's inheritance, so that they won't be in charge of investing and spending any money you leave them until they're responsible adults
- completed a will or decided to complete a living trust to make your choices legally binding
- reviewed your retirement plans and life insurance policies to make sure that you're leaving enough behind and leaving it to the right people in the right way, and
- chosen people to make critical health care and financial decisions for you if you're ever too sick to make them for yourself.

What You Just Did: Handy Estate Planning Summary	
Here are the documents you may have in your estate plan and why you have them.	
Will	Names guardians for minor children and leaves your assets to your spouse first and then to your children. It also establishes a trust to manage the money that your children might inherit from you.
Living Trust	Holds your assets so that they will pass to your spouse and children without having to go through probate.
Health Care Directives	Names an agent to make health care decisions for you if you are incapacitated; states your wishes for end-of-life care.
Durable Power of Attorney for Finances	Names an agent who can take care of your property if you're incapacitated.
Beneficiary Designation Forms: Retirement and Life Insurance Policies (you'll have copies; originals go to the institutions that manage these assets)	Names your primary and alternate beneficiaries.

Storing Your Estate Plan

Now what? First, you'll need a safe place to store your estate planning documents. You probably don't want to store your will or trust in a bank's safe deposit box, because it would be difficult for your family to get into the box after your death. Instead, put your original signed documents (and copies of your beneficiary forms) in a fireproof box. You can buy these at office supply stores and big-box retailers. Then tell your family where it is—and how to open it.

Whom to Give Copies To

Second, you might want to make copies of your documents and give them to the executor of your will and trustee of your trust. You don't have to, though. During your lifetime, no one has to see your plan. Everything you've decided is completely confidential. If you want to share your plan, of course, that's fine. If you don't, you probably have a good reason.

I would recommend making copies of your health care directives and your durable power of attorney for finances. Give a copy of each to the agents you've chosen for health care and property. If you're in a car accident or other emergency, they'll need those documents right away. Also give a copy of your health directives to your doctor, so that it will be in your medical records file.

Keeping Your Plan Current

You're going to have review and revise your plan occasionally—probably every three to five years, or when something major happens in your lives or the lives of your guardians, executors, or trustees. Even though you've worked hard to make good decisions, the odds that you'll never have to review or revise your estate plan during your lifetime are practically zero.

> **EXAMPLE:** Tim and Leslie made an estate plan five years ago. Since then they've had a baby, bought a house, and started a business. It's time for them to revise their existing plan.

When to Update Your Plan

Here are a few of the most common reasons that people revise their estate plans.

You have more children. Asking someone to be the guardian of one child can be different from asking them to raise two or three children.

Your children get older. As they do, your choices for guardians are likely to change. Perhaps your children want to stay closer to home; perhaps they've grown close to a relative you didn't name as guardian when they were little; perhaps your guardians are getting too old to handle teenagers.

Guardians, trustees, or executors move far away. When the people you've chosen to take care of things move away, you might need to choose people closer to home.

You have a falling out with your guardians, trustees, or executors. Friendships end; siblings quarrel. Sometimes that means you have to make new choices.

Your guardians get divorced or remarry. If your guardians change their family situation, you might want to rethink your choices.

You get divorced or remarry. In either case, you'll have to review your will, trust, beneficiary designations, and life insurance needs.

You move to another state. Estate planning is state law-specific. You want to make sure that you have a will or trust, as well as durable powers of attorney and health care directives, that are valid where you live.

Here are three state-specific issues to watch out for:

- **Custodial gifts to minors.** A couple of states haven't adopted the Uniform Transfers to Minors Acts, so you might need to revise how you've left minors money in the care of a custodian. And different states require custodianships to end at different ages.

- **Marital property.** If you move from a community property state to a common law state or vice versa, and don't intend to leave half of everything to your spouse, you will need to get an attorney's help to make sure your plan is drafted properly under your new state's rules.

- **Domestic partners.** If you move from a state that recognizes the rights of domestic partners to a state that does not or vice versa, you should get an attorney's help to review your existing plan to make sure that you're taking care of each other properly.

- **Your financial situation changes.** You inherit money. Your company goes public. You get fired. You go bankrupt. Good or bad, a big financial change usually means that you should review your estate plan to see whether your choices still make sense.

What Next? Storing and Reviewing Your Estate Plan

Storage. Keep your estate planning documents in a safe, fireproof box. Tell your family where it is and how to open it.

Copies. Make copies of your health care directive and your durable power of attorney for property management. Give a copy to the agents you've named in those documents. If you want, make a copy of your will or trust and give it to your executor or trustee.

Review. Review your estate plan every three to five years, and update it whenever something major changes in your lives or the lives of your guardians, trustees, or executors.

How to Make Changes to Your Estate Plan

When you need to make changes to your estate planning documents you can't just cross out a name, write in a new one, and initial the margin. Judges hate that. They won't know who made the mark, when it was made, or whether you really intended to make that change. (Remember evil nephew Fred?) Instead, you need to formally make changes and revoke your old documents. Here's how.

Updating Your Will

If you decide to make changes to your will, you can probably do so easily. If you've done your own will, just make a new one. If a lawyer drafted your will, ask them to make you a new one. The second sentence of a will usually says that you revoke any previous wills. That means that your most current will is the only valid one. Make sure to destroy your old wills, so there's no confusion about which one is the newest version.

Another way to update your will is to add what's called a "codicil" to it. A codicil states the changes you want to make to the original will. Because you must sign and witness a codicil, it's almost always a better idea just to make a new will. It's not much more work, and that way your changes are integrated into one document, which makes it easier to read and harder to lose.

EXAMPLE: Craig and Laura wrote a will after their first child was born, naming Laura's sister Anne as the guardian. When Craig and Laura have twins five years later, they decide that they need to pick a new guardian. Anne, by then, is a single mom with two children of her own, living in a small apartment.

Craig and Laura write a new will, naming Craig's younger brother, Jim, as the guardian for their three children. Jim has one child of his own and a 20-acre ranch, so they feel that he would be better able to take on three more children. They also increase the value of their term life insurance policy so that there would be more money available to raise all three kids.

Updating Your Living Trust

If you've got a living trust, you usually can amend just the sections of it that you want to change, without revoking the whole thing and starting over. (It's more trouble to revoke a trust than it is to revoke a will, because if you make a new trust you have to transfer property out of the old one and into the new.)

If, for example, you want to name a new trustee, you can amend the paragraph that names trustees and leave the rest of the trust alone. If you did a trust yourself, the software or book that you used should also include an amendment form that you can print out and sign in front of a notary. You'd then keep the amendment with the original trust document and make sure that anyone who had a copy of the trust also gets a copy of the amendment.

If you worked with an estate planner, ask that lawyer to make the amendment. Most estate planners charge on an hourly basis for amendments. If all you're doing is a simple change of a trustee or something similar, an amendment shouldn't take more than an hour of the lawyer's time.

> **TIP**
>
> **Sometimes a simple amendment can cost more than you think.** If you ask an attorney to amend a trust that he or she didn't draft in the first place, you might find it's an expensive proposition. A new lawyer must thoroughly review an existing document before making even a simple change. That's because a lawyer who amends a document is on the hook for any mistakes in the original. So you'll be paying for at least a couple of hours of a new lawyer's time. It's always less expensive to go back to the lawyer who wrote the trust the first time.

Updating Powers of Attorney and Health Care Directives

Keeping your powers of attorney and health care directives up to date usually means making sure you're still comfortable with the agents you've chosen and that your documents are valid for the state where you now live.

If you need to make new documents, just make sure to revoke the existing ones and tear them up. A revocation can be a simple document stating that you are revoking your existing durable power of attorney or health directive, dated _____, 20xx, and executing a new one. After you've created new documents, make sure to give them to the people you gave copies of the old one to, and get them to destroy the old ones as well.

Updating Beneficiary Designations and Insurance

To update your retirement, life insurance, or payable-on-death beneficiary designations, you'll need to request and fill out a change of beneficiary designation. (You can get the forms from the company that holds the asset or issued the policy.) Make sure to keep a copy of these forms with your will, trust, and powers of attorney documents so that your family will know that you've updated them.

That's it. You're done. Now take your kids to the park.

■

How to Use the CD-ROM

Many of the forms and worksheets discussed in the book are included on a CD-ROM in the back of the book. This CD-ROM, which can be used with Windows computers, installs files that you use with software programs that are already installed on your computer. It is *not* a standalone software program. Please read this appendix and the README.TXT file included on the CD-ROM for instructions on using the Forms CD.

Note to Mac users: This CD-ROM and its files should also work on Macintosh computers. Please note, however, that Nolo cannot provide technical support for non-Windows users.

How to View the README File

If you do not know how to view the file README.TXT, insert the Forms CD-ROM into your computer's CD-ROM drive and follow these instructions:

- Windows 2000, XP, or Vista: (1) On your PC's desktop, double click the My Computer icon; (2) double click the icon for the CD-ROM drive into which the Forms CD-ROM was inserted; (3) double click the file README.TXT.
- Macintosh: (1) On your Mac desktop, double click the icon for the CD-ROM that you inserted; (2) double click the file README.TXT.

While the README file is open, print it out by using the Print command in the File menu.

Two types of files are contained on the CD-ROM:

- A word processing (RTF) form that you can open, complete, print, and save with your word processing program (see "Using the Word Processing Files to Create Documents," below), and
- MP3 audio files that you can listen to using your computer's media or MP3 player (see "Listening to the Audio Files," below).

See below for a list of forms, their file names, and their file formats.

> ### Listening Without Installing
>
> If you don't want to copy 24.2 MB of audio files to your hard disk, you can play the CD on your computer. For details, see "Playing the Audio Files Without Installing," below.

Installing the Form Files Onto Your Computer

Word processing forms that you can open, complete, print, and save with your word processing program (see "Using the Word Processing Files to Create Documents," below) are contained on the CD-ROM. Before you can do anything with the files on the CD-ROM, you need to install them onto your hard disk. In accordance with U.S. copyright laws, remember that copies of the CD-ROM and its files are for your personal use only.

Insert the Forms CD and do the following.

Windows 2000, XP, and Vista Users

Follow the instructions that appear on the screen. (If nothing happens when you insert the Forms CD-ROM, then (1) double click the My Computer icon; (2) double click the icon for the CD-ROM drive into which the Forms CD-ROM was inserted; (3) double click the file WELCOME.EXE.)

By default, all the files are installed to the \Busy Family Toolkit folder in the \Program Files folder of your computer. A folder called "Busy Family Toolkit" is added to the "Programs" folder of the Start menu.

Macintosh Users

Step 1: If the "Busy Family Toolkit CD" window is not open, open it by double clicking the "Busy Family Toolkit CD" icon.

Step 2: Select the "Busy Family Toolkit" folder icon.

Step 3: Drag and drop the folder icon onto the icon of your hard disk.

Using the Word Processing Files to Create Documents

This section concerns the files for forms that can be opened and edited with your word processing program.

All word processing forms come in rich text format. These files have the extension ".RTF." For example, the form for the Family Inventory discussed in Chapter 2 is on the file Inventory.rtf. All forms, their file names, and their file formats are listed below.

RTF files can be read by most recent word processing programs including all versions of MS Word for Windows and Macintosh, WordPad for Windows, and recent versions of WordPerfect for Windows and Macintosh.

To use a form from the CD to create your documents you must: (1) open a file in your word processor or text editor; (2) edit the form by filling in the required information; (3) print it out; (4) rename and save your revised file.

The following are general instructions. However, each word processor uses different commands to open, format, save, and print documents. Please read your word processor's manual for specific instructions on performing these tasks.

Do not call Nolo's technical support if you have questions on how to use your word processor or your computer.

Step 1: Opening a File

There are three ways to open the word processing files included on the CD-ROM after you have installed them onto your computer:

- Windows users can open a file by selecting its "shortcut" as follows: (1) Click the Windows "Start" button; (2) open the "Programs" folder; (3) open the "Busy Family Toolkit" subfolder; (4) open the "Forms" subfolder; (5) click the shortcut to the form you want to work with.

- Both Windows and Macintosh users can open a file directly by double clicking it. Use My Computer or Windows Explorer (Windows 2000, XP, or Vista) or the Finder (Macintosh) to go to the folder you installed or copied the CD-ROM's files to. Then, double click the specific file you want to open.

- You can also open a file from within your word processor. To do this, you must first start your word processor. Then, go to the File menu and choose the Open command. This opens a dialog box where you will tell the program (1) the type of file you want to open (*.RTF) and (2) the location and name of the file (you will need to navigate through the directory tree to get to the folder on your hard disk where the CD's files have been installed).

Where Are the Files Installed?

Windows users: RTF files are installed by default to a folder named Busy Family Toolkit\Forms in the \Program Files folder of your computer.

Macintosh users: RTF files are located in the "Forms" folder within the "Busy Family Toolkit" folder.

Step 2: Editing Your Document

Fill in the appropriate information according to the instructions and sample agreements in the book. Underlines are used to indicate where you need to enter your information, frequently followed by instructions in brackets. Be sure to delete the underlines and instructions from your edited document. You will also want to make sure that any signature lines in your completed documents appear on a page with at least some text from the document itself.

Editing Forms That Have Optional or Alternative Text

Some of the forms have optional or alternative text:

- With optional text, you choose whether to include or exclude the given text.
- With alternative text, you select one alternative to include and exclude the other alternatives.

When editing these forms, we suggest you do the following:

Optional text

If you *don't want* to include optional text, just delete it from your document.

If you *do want* to include optional text, just leave it in your document.

In either case, delete the italicized instructions.

Alternative text

First delete all the alternatives that you do not want to include, then delete the italicized instructions.

Step 3: Printing Out the Document

Use your word processor's or text editor's "Print" command to print out your document.

Step 4: Saving Your Document

After filling in the form, use the "Save As" command to save and rename the file. Because all the files are "read-only," you will not be able to use the "Save" command. This is for your protection. If you save the file without renaming it, the underlines that indicate where you need to enter your information will be lost, and you will not be able to create a new document with this file without recopying the original file from the CD-ROM.

Listening to the Audio Files

This section explains how to use your computer's media player to listen to the audio files. All audio files are in MP3 format. (Most computers come with a media player that plays MP3 files.) For example, "Interview with Author" is on the file LizaWeimanHanks. mp3. At the end of this appendix, you'll see a list of the audio files and their file names.

You can listen to files that you have installed on your computer, or you can listen without having installed the files to your hard disk. (See "Playing the Audio Files Without Installing," below.)

Please keep in mind that these are general instructions—because every media player is unique, these steps may not mirror the steps you need to follow to use your player. Please do not contact Nolo's technical support if you are having difficulty using your media player.

Listening to Audio Files You've Installed on Your Computer

There are two ways to listen to the audio files that you have installed on your computer:

- Windows users can open a file by selecting its "shortcut" as follows: (1) Click the Windows "Start" button; (2) open the "Programs" folder; (3) open the "Busy Family Toolkit" subfolder; (4) open the "Audio" subfolder; (5) click the shortcut to the audio segment you want to hear.

- Both Windows and Macintosh users can open a file directly by double clicking it. Use My Computer or Windows Explorer (Windows 2000, XP, or Vista) or the Finder (Macintosh) to go to the folder in which you installed or copied the CD-ROM's files. Then, double click the MP3 file you want to hear.

Playing the Audio Files Without Installing

If you don't want to copy 24.2 MB of audio files to your hard disk, you can "play" the CD on your computer. Here's how.

Windows Users

Step 1: Insert the Forms CD to view the "Welcome to Busy Family Toolkit CD" window. (If nothing happens when you insert the Forms CD-ROM, double click the My Computer icon, double click the icon for the CD-ROM drive into which the Forms CD-ROM was inserted, and double click the file WELCOME.EXE.)

Step 2: Click "Listen to Audio."

Mac Users

Step 1: Insert the Forms CD. If the "Busy Family Toolkit CD" window does not open, open it by double clicking the "Busy Family Toolkit CD" icon.

Step 2: Open the "Audio" folder by double clicking the "Audio" icon.

Step 3: Double click the audio file you want to hear.

Forms Included on the Forms CD-ROM

The following files are in rich text format (RTF):

Form Title	File Name
The Ideal Guardian	IdealGuardian.rtf
Potential Guardians	PotentialGuardian.rtf
Guardians for My Children	KidsGuardian.rtf
Family Inventory	Inventory.rtf
My Children's Money Managers	MoneyManagers.rtf
Inheritance Planner	InheritPlan.rtf
How Much Could the Kids Inherit?	InheritMuch.rtf
Property Guardians for My Children	PropertyGuardian.rtf
My Executors	Executor.rtf
Will Worksheet	WillWorksheet.rtf
Will	Will.rtf
How to Sign Your Will	HowToWill.rtf
Family Retirement Assets: Current Beneficiaries	Assets.rtf
My Health Care Agent	HealthAgent.rtf
My Agent for Financial Management	FinancialAgent.rtf

The following file is audio (MP3):

Form Title	File Name
Interview with Author Liza Hanks: Guardianship Issues	FAM1_Guardianship.MP3
An Interview with author Liza Hanks: Family Assets and Leaving Money to Children	FAM2_Assets.MP3
Scenario: A couple with two children meets with an estate planning attorney.	FAM_Scenario.MP3

Index

Get the Latest in the Law

 Nolo's Legal Updater
We'll send you an email whenever a new edition of your book is published!
Sign up at **www.nolo.com/legalupdater**.

 Updates at Nolo.com
Check **www.nolo.com/update** to find recent changes in the law that
affect the current edition of your book.

 Nolo Customer Service
To make sure that this edition of the book is the most recent one, call us at
800-728-3555 and ask one of our friendly customer service representatives
(7:00 am to 6:00 pm PST, weekdays only). Or find out at **www.nolo.com**.

 Complete the Registration & Comment Card ...
... and we'll do the work for you! Just indicate your preferences below:

- -

Registration & Comment Card

NAME _____ DATE _____

ADDRESS _____

CITY _____ STATE _____ ZIP _____

PHONE _____ EMAIL _____

COMMENTS _____

WAS THIS BOOK EASY TO USE?   (VERY EASY)   5   4   3   2   1   (VERY DIFFICULT)

☐ Yes, you can quote me in future Nolo promotional materials. *Please include phone number above.*

☐ Yes, send me **Nolo's Legal Updater** via email when a new edition of this book is available.

Yes, I want to sign up for the following email newsletters:

  ☐ **NoloBriefs** (monthly)
  ☐ **Nolo's Special Offer** (monthly)
  ☐ **Nolo's BizBriefs** (monthly)
  ☐ **Every Landlord's Quarterly** (four times a year)

☐ Yes, you can give my contact info to carefully selected
partners whose products may be of interest to me.

FAM 1.0

NOLO

Nolo
950 Parker Street
Berkeley, CA 94710-9867
www.nolo.com

YOUR LEGAL COMPANION